Like a Haystack

Life from My Perspective

Margaret Grgurić Smolik

Copyright © 2014 Margaret Grgurić Smolik.

All rights reserved. No part of this book may be used or reproduced by any means, graphic, electronic, or mechanical, including photocopying, recording, taping or by any information storage retrieval system without the written permission of the publisher except in the case of brief quotations embodied in critical articles and reviews.

WestBow Press books may be ordered through booksellers or by contacting:

WestBow Press
A Division of Thomas Nelson & Zondervan
1663 Liberty Drive
Bloomington, IN 47403
www.westbowpress.com
1 (866) 928-1240

Because of the dynamic nature of the Internet, any web addresses or links contained in this book may have changed since publication and may no longer be valid. The views expressed in this work are solely those of the author and do not necessarily reflect the views of the publisher, and the publisher hereby disclaims any responsibility for them.

Any people depicted in stock imagery provided by Thinkstock are models, and such images are being used for illustrative purposes only. Certain stock imagery © Thinkstock.

ISBN: 978-1-4908-4035-2 (sc)
ISBN: 978-1-4908-4034-5 (hc)
ISBN: 978-1-4908-4036-9 (e)

Library of Congress Control Number: 2014910472

Printed in the United States of America.

WestBow Press rev. date: 7/10/2014

Contents

Preface vii

Part 1: Life in Yugoslavia and Austria: World War II Era

Land and Politics 3
Family Background 7
Theresa's Account 10
Life in Lahrndorf, Austria 24
    Daily Chores 28
    Holiday Celebrations 32
        Old Saint Nick and the Devil 32
        Christmas 33
        Easter 35
    Escargot and Other Strange Delicacies 36
    Grandparents 39
Garsten 42
    School in Garsten 44
    National Holidays 49
Steyr and Enns 52

Part 2: A New Land

The Trip to America 57
Ossian, Iowa 59

Roseville, Iowa 62
    Saint Mary's Church and School 64
    One-Room School (1952–1954) 67
The Move to Des Moines, Iowa 70
    Saint Joseph Academy 74
    Balancing Work and Fun 78
    Religious Training..81

Final Thoughts..85
    Theresa and Rosi...87
Epilogue..91
Appendix 93

Preface

Despite frequent encouragement from friends, I delayed writing the story of my childhood because it seemed an overwhelming task. I questioned the value of such an attempt since many early memories are vague and much of what I know comes secondhand through family and others who had experienced the horrors of World War II. I also thought that how we lived and what we endured described thousands of families, and we were not so different. However, the more years that go by since WWII, the more unusual my family's story becomes.

I came to realize that I could write a few stories that, taken together, would provide a fairly accurate overview of my early life and the trivial and important events that shaped me. However, in the course of writing, a larger story took shape, and the result is more comprehensive than anything I had anticipated. Multiple conversations with my oldest sister and a little research put flesh on bare bones and created a more complete, three-dimensional picture of my life.

I hope that my family, friends, and other readers will find something of interest in these pages. Those who know me will come to understand me better, learn what life was like in mid-twentieth-century Europe, and appreciate the difficulties of bridging several cultures.

I am well aware that my story will go to the grave with me if I do not share it. World War II and its aftermath are just historical events for many people, but they are reality for those of us affected by them. Their influences are lifelong, yet we ourselves often are not aware of the extent to which certain influences shape our personalities and our worldview. I am both a casualty and a survivor.

Survival, I have come to learn, is more difficult than accepting new people, ideas, and habits. It is affected by the tension that results from differences in the adjustment process by the individuals involved. Undercurrents of dissatisfaction and clashes between old and new never go away; they continue to affect family relationships and one's sense of peace, comfort, and feeling "at home." The impact, I believe, is greater for children than their parents. The children must navigate between the extremes of two worlds.

The story begins in Croatia, the land of my family's birth, moves to Austria, our home for seven years, and ends in America, in Iowa.

Part I

Life in Yugoslavia and Austria: World War II Era

LAND AND POLITICS

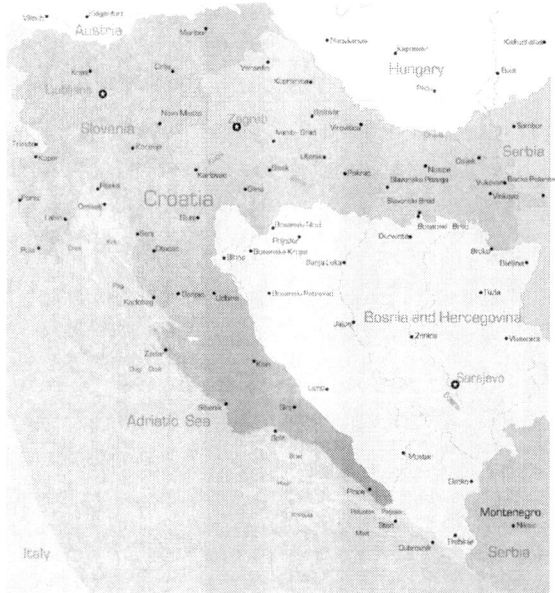

Map of Croatia

ACROSS THE ADRIATIC SEA FROM Italy lies a country known for the beauty of its coastline, its varied climate, its Alpine ruggedness, and its importance as the breadbasket of its people.

Croatia is a small country of approximately fifty-six thousand square miles (about the size of West Virginia) and a population of 4.5 million people situated below Hungary and Austria in southeastern Europe. It curves down the Adriatic coast for over a thousand miles and claims more than a thousand islands that rival the French Riviera in their breathtaking splendor. The Southern Alps, or Dinaric Alps, span much of the country and are among the most rugged and mountainous of any Alpine regions. Green forests and waterfalls abound and add to the beauty of the land.

Because of its location, Croatia has diverse climates influenced by the Alps and the Mediterranean Sea, which lies directly to the south. The Mediterranean zone, the north and west parts of the country, has mild to hot summers and moderate winters; the continental zone toward the north and east has greater temperature variations that allow snow each year and adequate summer rains. That is of great benefit to Slavonia, one of the seven regions that make up the country. Slavonia consists mostly of flat and fertile land in the valleys of the Danube, Drava, and Sava rivers and so is an important source of food for all of Croatia.

For more than seventy years, roughly 1920–1990, Croatia was part of the country of Yugoslavia, not independent as it is now. The Croats, Serbs, Slovenes, and other nations were combined after World War I into the Kingdom of Yugoslavia. Croatia, then as now, was approximately 90 percent Roman Catholic. The other 10 percent included Christians of various denominations, Orthodox Christians, and Muslims. Orthodox Christians and Muslims were more prominent in other parts of Yugoslavia. Religious expression was very important to all of them, but religious strife was minimal for many years.

In March 1941, under threat of invasion, the Yugoslav government signed a cooperation treaty with Nazi Germany to allow German troops to move through Yugoslavia toward Greece. However, the treaty was extremely unpopular and denounced by many. In response, Hitler swore to wipe Yugoslavia off the map and invaded the country in April 1941. Many willing collaborators helped Hitler, but resistance movements sprang up to challenge the occupation, and over the next three to four years, conflicts and ethnic cleansing raged across the country. In Croatia, hundreds of thousands of Jews, Serbs, and gypsies were killed.

One cannot understand the violence without some idea of the four major factions within the country. The *domobrane* were members of the legitimate Croatian army. The *ćetniks* consisted of those who wanted to retain the monarchy that ruled Yugoslavia. The *partisane* were the military arm of the Communist Party of Yugoslavia whose primary goal was to create a Communist state. Its commander was Josip Broz Tito. The most violent were the *ustaśe*, a Croatian fascist and terrorist organization responsible for the deaths of thousands of citizens. The supporters of the ustaśe blended Nazism and nationalism in their desire to create a Greater Croatia, especially a racially "pure" Croatia. They promoted persecution and genocide against Serbs, Jews, and Roma (gypsies). Sad to say, many of them were also fanatically Catholic.

When Josip Broz Tito, a member of the partisan party, came to power in the late 1930s and early 1940s, he ruled with an iron fist. He tried to suppress nationalist sentiment and promote greater unity among the six Yugoslav nations. He forbade or tightly controlled the overt practice of religion and religious ceremonies among all religious groups. Despite what critics might say, Tito was the only leader aligned with Russia to defy Soviet control. He wanted to follow independent roads to socialism, and because of this nonalignment, he remained independent of the two hostile blocs in the Cold War––the East and the West. He greatly influenced the Yugoslav economic recovery of the 1960s and 1970s.

This general overview of Croatia provides important background to better understand the times and events described below. While not directly related to Croatia, I want to describe an important battle in Germany that is referred to later in the account of my family's history.

One of the most horrific attacks of the war was the Allied powers' fire bombing of Dresden, Germany. On the evening of February 13, 1945, approximately seven to eight hundred British bombers dropped three thousand high-explosive bombs on the city. In the second wave, which included American bombers, more than five hundred thousand highly flammable bombs were dropped on the city to burn out buildings and inhabitants. A firestorm that generated hurricane winds raged throughout the city. In three days of bombing, at least 135,000 lives were lost.

This was the single most destructive bombing of the war––including Hiroshima and Nagasaki. However, the reasons for bombing Dresden have never been clear. Allied forces bombed strategic German cities known for war production, but Dresden was not one of these. It was a beautiful medieval city known for its art and architectural treasures.

I cry when I see pictures of Dresden and other such cities. My family was there just prior to the bombing, and we were fortunate to have left in time. The horrors of war should make us committed to solving world problems in ways other than with guns and bombs.

Family Background

My family traces its roots to the fertile plains of Slavonia, a region in eastern Croatia. We come from the town of Voćin. It was a small town of two or three thousand people, and we lived on a farm with our grandparents, Franjo (Frank) and Marija (Mary) Wahl, on a street called Prevenda. Grandfather and Grandmother Wahl had only one daughter, Teresija (Theresa), my mother, born in 1920.

Grandpa was a hardworking farmer who had two teams of horses to plow the few acres of land he owned. He hired one man, sometimes two, to take care of the horses and help with other chores. In addition to planting, harvesting, and raising farm animals, Grandpa and Grandma had a meat market, and they butchered cattle and hogs for the family and for others when there was a need. They opened a restaurant and bar on weekends and prepared most of the food. Saturday evenings usually included music and dancing. Also, a local businessman sometimes hired Grandpa and a team of his horses and a wagon to go to the forest nearby for loads of lumber that were taken to the railroad and shipped out.

There was always work to do, and Mother, the only child (a sibling had died in childbirth), was given much responsibility at an early age. For example, when she was only nine, she was left alone to milk the cows, feed the livestock, and do other chores while her parents were gone for the day to deliver lumber. She worked hard in the kitchen to cook not only for the family but also for the hired hands when necessary. She did her share in the garden and fields as well. Mom did not talk much about her growing-up years. Perhaps they were normal for the time, but certainly her parents expected much. Although she liked to laugh and dance, Mom grew up to be a rather serious, no-nonsense person.

In 1935, at the age of fifteen, Mom married my father, Franjo Grgurić, who was twenty-two years old. Dad, a tall, handsome, blue-eyed man, liked to tell stories and have a good time. I assume he learned to polka and waltz as a youngster, and I like to imagine him being taken to the dance floor by his mother or other women who taught him these and other common dances. Family gatherings, wedding receptions, and public dances were perfect opportunities to pass on a cultural heritage. That is how my sisters and I learned.

It is very likely that Mom and Dad met at a dance, perhaps at one of Grandpa's Saturday evening dances or at a local celebration. The town of Voćin was a center of activity. It hosted carnivals that drew people from the surrounding communities, and the beautiful church in town, dedicated to the Virgin Mary, was a popular destination for pilgrimages attended by parishioners and people from far away.

At the time they met, Dad worked for a local miller. In fact, from the age of twelve, when he left home, he was apprenticed to several men who operated flour mills along streams where farmers took their grain––corn, wheat, oats, and rye––to be ground into flour, coarse or fine, depending on its use. Dad lived with the families of the owners who provided room and board. After moving around, he settled in the Voćin area, far from his family. Interestingly, one of my father's teachers strongly recommended that he be allowed to continue his education after grade six because she could see possibilities in him. But earning a living at an early age was deemed more important by his parents, so Dad was denied the benefits of education just like my mother was.

After they married, Dad worked on Grandpa's farm, and Mother's responsibilities grew the more children she had. She was only sixteen when Teresia (Theresa) was born in 1936. Ružica (Rose) came along in 1939, and I, Greta (Margaret), was born in 1942. One of the stories Mom told me once surprised me. When she was needed in the fields, she took me along, placed me on a blanket at the end of a row under the shade of a tree, hoed and weeded to the other end, and nursed me when she made her way back.

Rosi's health during her early childhood was a major concern for Mom and Dad. Rosi became severely ill and had long bouts of high fever. The local doctor, it seems, could not heal her. A doctor might not even have been available since many were needed to treat wounded soldiers. On two occasions, Mom and Dad thought Rosi had died and were ready to light candles and call the priest. Rosi recovered, but throughout her life she did not have the strength and stamina that most children have.

All three of us were born during the time of Hitler's rise to power, which began in 1933 and lasted through the Second World War, 1939–1945. Since I was a baby when many events happened, I have had to rely on the stories and reminiscences of my parents and older sisters, especially Theresa, for details about what life was like and how that changed with the outbreak of World War II. Although I do not remember my earliest years, I do know that the person I am today is a product of those years. No one, babe or adult, escaped the devastating events of that time or survived unscathed, physically or emotionally. While I heard the stories many times, the early history described in the next section is based on my sister Theresa's recollections.

Theresa's Account

We lived in the Catholic section of Voćin. We could see our church and Calvary Hill from our house. The name of our church was Sveta Gospa, meaning Holy Lady. It was a very famous church, and during the year, the parish held several processions on holy days of obligation. People came from far away to attend; most of them had to walk. Some walked a whole day and found a place to sleep so they would be on time to attend Mass and join the processions. There were no buses, and the train was too expensive. Even if a family had a horse and wagon, they were not used for pleasure.

We lived with our grandparents. Grandpa and Grandma had two sets of horses and a wagon and two hired hands to help with all the work. Most of the thirty-three hectares of land (eighty-eight acres) were cultivated. They grew corn, wheat, oats, beans, poppies, and potatoes. Grandpa had a plow and a rake, but the planting was all done by hand. With a bag hanging around his neck full of either wheat or oats, Grandpa walked through the fields, grabbed a handful, and spread it out. When the bag was empty, he walked back to the wagon, filled his bag, and continued until the job was finished.

Grandpa planted corn by making a hole with a hoe, dropping a seed or two into it, and covering it. Sometimes he dropped in one seed of corn and one seed of pole beans. In this way, the beans had something to climb on, and then picking the beans was much easier than bending to the ground. Green beans were picked as needed. Ripe beans were picked and put on a big pile. When all picking and work was done for the season and the weather turned cold, the family and sometimes friends gathered to remove the beans from the dry shells. Those were fun evenings.

Our house was quite large. We used only one floor as living quarters; above that was only storage. The kitchen was the focal point for the family. In the left corner was the brick stove and beyond that a few shelves for dishes and a table for kitchen work. The right side of the room had a very long table and chairs so the family and all hired hands could sit down. Mom did not have many dishes, but what she had were always put to good use, especially at harvest time. During harvest time when Grandpa had several people help in the fields, it was too time consuming to ask all the people to come back to the house for a meal. So Mom cooked the meal, left the food in the pots that it was cooked in, loaded the pots into a woven basket, put it on top of her head, and carried it to the field.

The very large bedroom that we used for the whole family was off the kitchen to the left. It had a bed in each corner and freestanding closets. All of us slept in there. In the winter, we opened the door so the heat would come in from the kitchen. There was no other way to heat that room. The other two bedrooms were to the right of the kitchen. Each had its own outside entrance. Both were empty, but one had a ladder that we climbed to get to the attic. There we had wooden containers in which we kept poppy seeds used for baking only. I also believe that after we killed a pig and smoked some of the meat, we dragged it up to the attic and hung it there until we used it.

Across the yard was another house with an upstairs used for storing grain and such. The basement had to be entered around back and was used as an ice cellar. Grandpa was also a butcher, and every week he killed whatever he could buy from one of the nearby farmers. Some weeks he bought a cow, other weeks a pig or goat or sheep. He killed only one because there was no refrigeration, and leftover meat spoiled easily. During the winter, Grandma and Grandpa went to the river and cut out pieces of ice, stored them in the ice cellar, and then used the ice during the summer to preserve any meat that was not sold.

The animals that Grandpa bought for his shop had to be walked home. He walked from farmer to farmer and asked if he had anything he wanted to sell, and the farmer would either sell to him or tell him to come back in a week or two or a month. As he walked many miles, Grandpa observed different fruit trees. When he saw one that was special, he went back the next year and took a few small branches and grafted his own trees. He actually showed us how to do it when we visited him and Grandma many years later in Austria in 1975.

When harvest season was over, and Grandpa had some free time, he went to the river and brought back birch branches. He cut the big branches into smaller sticks, which he lined up so each stack would be the same size. He then took an old broom handle and tied the branches to the end of the stick to make a wonderful broom for cleaning the yard. In fact, after we arrived in Austria in 1943 or 1944, he made the same kind of brooms, and Dad would load them onto his back, walk from farmer to farmer, and exchange the brooms for food. The food I remember most is red beets, but I am sure he brought back other things too.

We left Voćin in early 1943. Dad was already gone by this time. He had to join the Domobrane (dom = home, brane = protect), the Croatian army, sometime in 1941. The Germans were bombing the Croatian sector, and weeks prior to our leaving, the fighting was intense as different factions, the domobrane, partisane, and ustaśe, fought not only the Germans but also each other. I remember when the shooting was loud and very near, Mom told me to sit on the floor so if any bullets came through the window they would not hit me. One day, a soldier was hit and could not walk. Enemy soldiers put him in a wheelbarrow, wheeled him down the street, and made him holler and call to his friends to give up or the same would happen to them. I also remember that a hand grenade landed on the roof of our house right above Mom's bed. It did not explode but just got stuck up there. It stayed in the attic as long as we lived there. I don't believe we ever found out what happened. At least my parents or grandparents never mentioned anything.

When the fighting got very intense in early 1943, the Germans came and said to Grandfather, "Because you are German, we will protect you for three more days. After that, you are on your own. So we suggest that you leave with your family." Because Grandpa's name was

Wahl, a German name, he was warned and given an opportunity not granted to everyone. I believe it was the following day that he got two of his younger horses and a wagon, put my ill mother––who had come down with typhoid fever of the stomach and of the head just prior to this––inside with a few belongings, and we left Voćin for good. On the wagon with us were Grandma's brother John, his wife and children, and several other people for a total of sixteen. However, we left a number of relatives behind in Voćin, like Grandpa's three sisters, Anna (Anuśka), Katie (Kata), and Mary (Mariśka), and their families.

Grandmother was also of German background. Her maiden name was Nadler, and she was born in Bokane only a few miles east from Voćin. She was one of eight children, the only girl. As mentioned earlier, her brother John lived in Voćin with his wife and two children, a boy and a girl. They also took in a young girl who helped with the work around the house. John was a tailor by trade. The other brothers lived in Bokane, and when the war broke out, they were all killed. In fact, my husband, Tony, when he was about eight years old, found one of them in the woods dismembered with parts of his body sticking out from under the leaves. Shortly after that, Tony and his parents left Bokane and never returned.

I cannot say for sure what and how much we left behind. I know much grain had been stored for the year, which we took to the miller and had ground into flour as we needed it. Several cows, some pigs, two horses, chickens, geese, and ducks were left behind as well as barrels of śljivovac (plum whiskey). We had a plum grove with probably a hundred plum trees. We also had our own distillery and made the "good stuff."

When we left, I was six years old, my sister Rose was three, and Margaret was eight months old. It was very hard for Mom because there was no baby food in jars. Most babies were breast fed until they were eighteen months old, but Mom had typhoid fever and could not feed Margaret any more. I do not know what she did for food. And it was not just food for Margaret; we all had to eat. I know that as we entered a town, there were designated people who showed us which house to drive to and enter the yard. The people there had to take us in, give us a room or two for sleeping, and feed us. We stayed with the people until the fighting came close and we all had to leave again. Some people refused to leave, but the authorities took Mom and the three of us girls and put us on a train to Dresden, Germany. Grandpa and Grandma took the horses and wagon and were told to move on to Feldkirchen, Austria. There, Grandpa worked for a farmer in exchange for food and a place to sleep. The train ride to Dresden was probably in 1944. We were there until shortly before the fire bombing of Dresden in February 1945.

When Mother and we girls got to Dresden, we were put up in a large building with many other displaced families; by that, I mean women and children. The rooms were filled with bunk beds, three high. I slept there only one night and the next day I was full of lice. Mom tried everything to get rid of them, but there was no way. Many of us children had lice mostly in our hair. My hair was very long and thick, so they had a good place to hide. Every day, Mom stood over me and tried to find the lice and kill them so they would not bite me, but it was to no avail. Eventually, our mothers put gasoline on our heads, rubbed it in well, and then wrapped our heads in turbans for a few days. I guess they thought that would kill the lice and the eggs. But when they took off the turbans, our hair was like an ant's nest. So we went back to the old ways of killing them one by one.

Aunt Katie (Grandpa's sister) and her children, Eddie and Olga, were in Dresden the same time we were. We were all lucky to get out three days prior to the American fire bombing of the city. The farmer that Grandpa worked for near Feldkirchen was kind enough to accept Mom and the three of us girls, so Grandpa went to town and got permission for us to move.

The first papers that Mom received telling us we were allowed to move were destroyed by the man in charge of the camp. You see, the story goes that at home he was nothing more than a sheepherder. At the camp, he was in charge of many people, and that gave him authority. As people were leaving, he realized that if all left, he would have to go back and be a sheepherder again, and he supposedly did not like that. Well,

LIKE A HAYSTACK

Grandpa made new papers; this time, Mom did not say anything to the man. She packed up our small bundle of nothing, and we left Dresden.

We arrived in Feldkirchen by train and lived at the farmhouse with my grandparents. All this time, we did not know where Dad was. Eventually, we found out that he had been taken prisoner by the Germans. After we were together again, he told us a scary story.

One particular day, the soldiers were at the train station, and a freight train came. The boxcars were loaded with people packed in like sardines. The soldiers were afraid to open the doors in case someone fell out. They begged for water, and Dad took his canteen and handed it to one of the people. They were so thirsty they grabbed the canteen and fought over it. Almost all the water spilled on their clothing, and they actually licked the water off each other. When a German soldier saw what Dad had done, he was very angry and wanted to shoot him right there. The people on the train were Jews, and that was the wrong thing for Dad to do.

We settled in by the farmer, and all looked okay, I guess. But we found out that we were in the Russian sector. The Russian soldiers started coming to the farm, and when they found out that Mom's name was Grgurić, a Croatian name, they insisted she go back to Jugoslavia. Not knowing where Dad was, still not feeling the best, and having to take three of us small children, she wondered what she would go back to. Since much killing was still going on among the various factions, what was waiting for her? She decided not to go, so every time we saw the soldiers coming, Mom ran and hid in the beet or potato field or wherever she felt safe. We'd go and find her after the soldiers left.

Because Grandpa still had his two horses on the farm, we were able to use them to go to Linz, the capital of the state of Upper Austria (Oberösterreich) located in the north-central part along the Danube River. Located near Linz were the last concentration camps liberated by Allied forces. After the war, Linz served as the border between the Russian and American occupation zones.

The farmer had a buggy, and Mom and Grandpa took Herman, the fast horse, and went to Linz, more than one hundred miles away, to visit Lager (camp) #65. The barracks were lined up one next to the other and filled with displaced people from all over. Mom and Grandpa tried to find someone they knew. They found out that we would be accepted into the camp like all the other people. They also found out about a man who could smuggle us out of the Russian to the American sector. The man had a pickup truck lined with boxes and in the middle was an opening. Grandma, one of my sisters, and I climbed in, pushed a box in to cover the hole, and we were on our way. Mom, Grandpa, and my other sister went to the Danube, and there a man with a small boat took them across the river. A rope was strung across to make sure they did not get carried down river. When they reached the other side, they joined us in Linz.

We were in Lager 65 for only a few days. Because there were so many people needing space, we were told to go to another camp in Asten, about fifteen miles away. Asten Lager was an American camp with forty or fifty barracks. We lived in Barrack 35; Barrack 34 was the school. I was about eight years old, and it was the first time in my life that I attended school. I was taught Cyrillic, the Russian alphabet, which is very different from the European alphabet.

After we moved to Asten, Mom finally found out that Dad was alive! The war was over——Germany officially surrendered in May 1945——and as men were coming home, they mentioned the names of men who were left behind in different places. Mom found out that Dad was in Austria in a town called Spital am Traun. To get there, she had to take the train, but fortunately, it was not too far away. She had no money, so how would she get him?

During the time we were in the camp, all grownups were given cigarettes. It did not matter if one smoked or not; each person got a ration. Grandpa smoked all of his, but Mom put hers away, and guess what? She used the cigarettes to pay her way to get Dad. She handed the conductor some cigarettes, and he allowed her to ride the train. Mom then brought Dad back to Camp Asten.

During the time Dad was gone, he was a prisoner in a camp and was wounded. A piece of shrapnel had hit his right arm just below his shoulder, and because there were no doctors, the wound got very infected. He told us that his arm was so swollen that it stuck straight out, and the wound was filled with so much pus that when he squeezed it, pus dropped out in chunks. I guess many men died. Finally, someone told one of the guards that there were many ill and wounded men inside this camp. They took all the sick ones out, and Dad was one of them. When he got to the hospital and the doctors were ready to operate on him, they were in such a hurry that they started to cut his wound before he was asleep. He told us he hollered so loud that they stopped and gave him more morphine.

While living in Camp Asten, Dad was janitor in the school barrack and Grandpa was the furnace man. While tending to the furnace, Grandpa also made brooms, which I mentioned before, and Dad took them to the farmers over the weekend and traded for food. Dad had other jobs as well; one of them was to clean one of the barracks used for entertaining the troops. As they were cleaning it out, they found some DDT powder. Dad came running home, gave Mom a folded napkin, and said, "Here is this teaspoon of white powder. Use it for getting rid of the lice." So the next thing I knew, I was sitting down, and Mom took a small pinch of this powder and rubbed it into my hair. This took care of every last one of them. I never had lice after that. What amazed all of us was that my sister Rose and I always slept together but she never had any lice.

We received rations once a day, mostly soup, and 99 percent of the time it was green pea soup. We were given a container according to the size of our family. Mom or Dad went to the kitchen, got some soup, and brought it home. We had to eat it because there was not much else.

We were at Camp Asten only six to nine months. The war was over by then (early to mid-1945), and all men were forced to find jobs. Dad and Grandpa both found work with a lumber firm called Weidinger located in Steyr, Austria. Some of the men worked in the forest, cutting down trees. Some brought the trees to the firm to be cut into boards. The company also produced prefabricated homes that were shipped to Italy and Greece. The homes had two bedrooms, a kitchen, and a very small foyer. They were not insulated, as they were just boards put together, which is why they could be used only in countries with warmer climates.

Dad rode his bicycle to work because of cost and the hours he worked. Some days he worked at the saw mill, but he could not be certain that work would be completed in time for him to take the evening train home. Other days he went into the mountains and helped bring back trees for the mill. The truck the men used had an extremely long bed—so long that it required a steering mechanism at the front and at the back. Dad usually drove the back end of the truck. The only way to make a curve around a mountain was to have someone turn the back steering wheel. He said that was hard. He had to turn the rear steering wheel in the opposite direction from the front one. He had a few close calls, but he did learn and was very good at it.

When Dad and Grandpa went to work for Mr. Weidinger, we were given a place to live in Lahrndorf, about four miles from Steyr. It was a barrack, and we, the seven of us, got two rooms. Mom, Dad, and we three girls slept in one room; Grandma and Grandpa slept in the other room, which was also our kitchen. Because the barrack was made from simple wood and had no insulation, it was very cold during the winter. The bedroom had no stove, so if we wanted to heat it a bit, we opened the door and let in some of the heat from the kitchen. However, we did not have much wood, so we had to watch how much we burned. If we used too much, there would be none to cook our meals. Grandpa, my sisters, and I walked through the woods, picked up branches, and brought them home in bundles.

Nine families lived in this barrack, and all had the same idea. To find enough branches, we had to walk quite a distance. We did this during colder weather; when the weather was warmer, Grandpa and I either went mushroom hunting, fishing, or begging. Yes, begging. Grandpa and I would walk almost all day, going from one farmer to the next, begging for food. Some farmers gave us one potato or two; some gave red beets and maybe other things that I no longer recall. Some gave nothing. But we did this for a long time until Dad and Grandpa started getting paid, and we could afford to buy food.

LIKE A HAYSTACK

We could fish only if the weather was quite warm. From our window, we could see the high mountains of the Alps that had snow on them year round. It was rather hilly where we lived with lots of trees, so the small river where we fished was quite cold. Grandpa wove a large basket and took along a long stick. We walked to the river; he took off his shoes, rolled up his pants, and stepped into the water. He put the basket on one side of a rock, took the stick, and poked on the other side. If a fish was hiding, it would try to swim away, and often one would swim into the basket. Grandpa then took the fish and threw it to me on shore (ha ha; the shore was nothing more than weeds five feet taller than I was), and I had to watch where he threw it so I could catch it and slide it on a stick through its gills. I walked with him until he got tired or felt that we had enough fish for us all to have a good supper.

We obviously had no refrigeration in those days. What Mom cooked had to be eaten the same day because we surely had no food to throw away. Winters were better. Dad put up a bench of sorts under our kitchen window, and that was used for food storage overnight. When we first came to Lahrndorf, Dad bought a couple of rabbits thinking they would multiply and we would have meat more than once a week. However, we had the rabbits for only a few days, and then they were gone. We never did find out who took them. Dad tried once more, and this time he bought a lock. The only food we had for the rabbits was grass. Every day, my sisters and I picked grass by hand so there would be enough until the next day. When school was in session, the first thing I did when I came home was pick grass before it got dark. Grandpa got a scythe somehow that he used to cut grass, and we made hay so we would have food for the rabbits in the winter.

None of the land was ours. It all belonged to Mr. Weidinger, but we were allowed to make use of it as we saw fit. Dad and Grandpa dug up a section, and Mom and Grandma made a garden. We had good, fresh food and did not have to go begging any more. The nine families in our barrack all did the same thing. We just had to share and help each other. Pots and pans were carried from one family to the other depending on what was being cooked.

When we first moved to Larhndorf, I, of course, had to go to school. The only schooling I had had so far was a week or two here or a month there. But because of our having to move all the time, I really had not learned a lot.

School was in Garsten, about four kilometers (two and a half miles) away, so I had to take the train every morning. I was put into third grade, and it was very hard. I could not speak German. I learned how to read only because Grandpa would take me on his lap and teach me. I knew my numbers but did not know any math. So I was in third grade for a few months, and then summer came. The next fall, I went to fourth grade. It was quite a challenge, to say the least.

After fourth grade, children had two choices: they could either go on to fifth, sixth, and seventh grades and be finished with school or go to high school. At first, my parents decided I should go the fifth grade route. But during fifth grade, Dad decided it would be better if I went to high school. I attended high school for four years, but before I could graduate, we finally got permission to go to America.

I left school sometime in January of 1952, and we arrived in America on February 19. I thank God for being so good to my parents and us children. Had we stayed in Austria, we would never have had the opportunity that we have had in America. One thing was sure: the Austrian people never accepted us. In their eyes, we were always the foreigners (Ausländer). My parents knew that when we finished school, no matter how many grades we had completed, we would wind up by a farmer and be nothing more than hired hands—what they called a barn maid (stallmensch). Many of our young girls and women wound up doing just that. Dad was not happy with that thought and worked very hard to get papers put together so we could go to America.

Displaced families were allowed to leave Austria and go to Australia, Canada, or the United States. How they decided who would go where I do not know. We did have permission to go to Australia, but Mom refused because she heard it took three weeks on the ship to get there and that people got very sick. She told Dad that if he wanted to go to do so, but she was not ready to die. Luckily, Dad found out that his uncle in Canada would take us in. In fact, he had built a two-unit apartment and said we could live in one unit. But when Dad approached the immigration people, they refused to let us come, saying that if they allowed people to go wherever they wanted, communists would be allowed to enter any country they wished, or something to that effect.

Dad worked on our going to the United States for three years. He had to leave his job in Steyr, take the bus to Asten about sixteen miles away, be there however long it took, and then come back to his job. There were many times when all of us had to go with him. We were given all kinds of injections and given the impression that we would go with the next group. However, three and a half years later, when Dad went to Asten again, a lady behind the desk called him to the side and asked him if he knew a man by the name of Adam L. "Yes," Dad said. "He lives in the same barrack where I live." He looked quite confused because he did not know what this had to do with our going to America. The lady explained that the man had gone to the American embassy and had reported Dad as being in the SS (Schutzstaffel, or protection squadron, Hitler's private army). Dad said, "Yes, I was, but not as an SS officer or soldier. I was taken prisoner." The lady told Dad to ask the man to go back to the embassy and tell them that he was wrong, that he had mistaken Dad for someone else. After Dad was given the news and told what to do, he returned to his job and finished his day.

He was quite late getting home that day because he worked longer to make up for lost hours. When he finally finished work, he had six kilometers to ride his bike. As I mentioned, we lived in a hilly area, so the ride to or from work was not very easy. Some hills were so steep we had to get off the bike and push it up the hill. And there were no lights along the road, which was all gravel and in some areas very narrow. Dad was about one kilometer from home in a very narrow ravine with room for only one vehicle when he almost fell over something. He came to a screeching halt and realized that a man and his bicycle were lying on the road. Dad tried to help the man and was surprised to find Mr. Adam L. himself, drunk as could be. If a vehicle had come along, he would have been dead. Dad picked him up, held him under the arm, took his own bike as well as Adam's, walked them home, and handed Adam over to his wife.

The next day was Saturday. When Dad went outside, he met Adam, who by then was half sober. Adam thanked Dad in a goofy way for bringing him home. Dad took the opportunity to ask him if he would be willing to go to the American consulate in Steyr to sign papers retracting his story. He did so, and a few days later, we got permission to go to America.

When our papers arrived, we had to leave quickly. During the years we tried getting permission to leave, many people said they would buy things from us. However, no one came forward to buy a single thing. We left everything behind but the clothes on our backs and a few belongings. I remember I had some books I just loved but could not take because we had no suitcases, and I could not just hold the books in my arms all the way to America.

We left Lahrndorf and stopped in Salzburg overnight. We slept in a dilapidated barrack in our clothes because there was no heat or covers. The next morning, we boarded a train to Bremerhaven, Germany. When we got there, Dad was told there was no more room on the ship going to New York so we would have to go to New Orleans. I think Dad would have accepted Siberia at this point.

We were one of the last few families that were part of the IRO (International Reorganization Organization) group. We boarded the U.S.S. General Blatchford and headed out to sea. It took us three weeks to get to New Orleans. The weather was bad for several days; in fact, ropes were strung out on deck for people to hang on to if they decided to go out. But not too many people went out, even on nice days. Many were quite seasick like my mother; she was in bed all three weeks.

Every corner had a large fifty-five gallon garbage can in case someone had to heave. Many people did, and the hallways stank like a garbage dump. Even if we were not seasick, the stench took care of that. Dad never did get sick; in fact, he was one of the workers on board. I was sick only a couple of days, but when I walked through the hallways, I ran just to get away from the dirty garbage cans or held my nose until I passed the stench.

The food on board ship was quite different from what we were used to, but when one cannot choose, one learns to like what one gets. It really was not bad, just different. I will never forget when I saw Jell-O for the first time. I could not figure out why they would cut jelly into pieces and serve it with lunch or supper. Jelly to me was a snack or filling for cookies. So, thinking that it was jelly, I tried putting it on my bread. Obviously, it did not work too well. It was then that the lady behind the counter explained to me how to eat Jell-O. Did I feel silly? Well, that is not the word! Looking back, I realize that was only the beginning of new things I had to learn.

LIFE IN LAHRNDORF, AUSTRIA

Map of Austria

I COULD NOT HAVE TOLD the story of my family in Yugoslavia or the experiences after we left there without Theresa, and I thank her for her help. Here begins my own account of what I remember and what I would like the reader to know about Austria and our early years in America. I hope the reader will understand that some of my memories overlap those of Theresa.

Lahrndorf, Austria, was a small town nestled in the north-central part of Austria in the state of Oberösterreich (Upper Austria) among the hills and valleys of the beautiful Alps. Surrounded by fields and farmsteads, the town was no more than a settlement that consisted of a train station, a house for the stationmaster, and several other houses strung along the tracks at some distance from each other. Trains went by twice a day, early morning and late afternoon, and provided transportation to school and work for people from the isolated hamlet that was Lahrndorf.

The building, or barrack, in which we lived was long and narrow, and a hallway ran down the center. The living quarters on either side of the hallway consisted of one- or two-room units, four or five on each side. Most of the people were refugees from other countries who had moved to Austria to escape the fighting. Each of the nine families was given an "apartment" depending on the number of family members. My family of seven—my parents, our grandparents, and we three girls—were given a two-room unit.

The door from the hallway opened into the kitchen. To the right of the door in the corner stood a small counter on which sat a basin or small bowl for washing hands, a pitcher of water, and a bar of homemade soap. A towel hung on a bar above it. Below the counter was a bucket for dirty water, a bucket for clean water, and a large basin for washing dishes. A floor-length fabric skirt attached around the outside of the counter covered the items under the bench. We carried water from an outside faucet for drinking, cooking, and washing dishes and clothes. If we needed hot water, we heated it on the stove.

To the left of the sink in the next corner was a bed on which my grandparents slept. A window to the left of the bed separated the "sleeping" area from the "dining" area. The dining area held an old wood table with a bench on one side and chairs around the other sides. It was the focal point for everything: eating meals; making dough for breads and pastries; sewing; shelling corn, peas, and beans; or studying. In the last corner, to the left of the entry door, stood a huge brick wood-burning cookstove with a cast-iron oven and cooking surface with three or four removable covers for direct heat. Next to the stove was a box that held kindling and large chunks of firewood.

A door between the stove and table led into an adjoining bedroom that had two beds, one for our parents and the other for my two sisters and me. Being the youngest, I had the middle position. Of course, we were cramped and had to learn to sleep quietly. We slept on mattresses stuffed with straw (and sometimes dry leaves) that had to be fluffed up every night. The thin layer of straw made the boards underneath feel only a little softer.

The room was very cold in the winter since there was no heat once the wood in the kitchen stove burned down. Thank God for feather pillows and comforters. Every chicken, goose, or duck we killed was plucked clean and the feathers saved. The large feathers were sorted and thrown away since they were too firm to use. Mother used some of the medium-sized feathers with the thinner quills to make pastry brushes. We stripped the feathers off the bottom half of the quills, and then mother wove them together tightly with strong thread. The top part of the brushes was soft and "feathery"—perfect for brushing dough and the tops of pastries with butter or egg whites. These brushes worked well and lasted a long time.

Pastry brush made with six or eight feathers tightly wound together

The small feathers and down were used to make pillows and comforters. During the winter when we were housebound, mother brought out the feathers, and for days we sat in the kitchen stripping feathers off even the smallest quills since the quills easily poked through the covers. Only the softest down could be left as it was. The bedding items Mother and Grandmother made helped us survive the cold of winter.

Not far from the barrack was an outhouse that served everyone. The first two or three units were reserved for the women and girls and the ones toward the back for the men and boys, but everyone entered and exited by the same door. Since the stalls had no doors, using the outhouse was a little embarrassing. We had no toilet paper, so we had to be creative. On the way to the *klo* (German for toilet), we found big leaves, pulled a fist full of grass, or came up with some other solution. If all we had to do was urinate, we just used our panties.

The outhouse was situated over a pit accessible from the outside. Each year, some men, including Dad and Grandpa, cleaned it out by scooping the manure into buckets and spreading it on people's gardens to fertilize them.

The barrack, we think, had housed workers during and after the war. Three nearby buildings were probably used to manufacture war supplies. When we moved to Lahrndorf, the buildings were empty and in bad shape. Most of the windows were broken, but the doors were locked, and no one was allowed inside. A faucet attached to one of the buildings was our main source of water. Another smaller brick building was situated within a few feet of the barrack. We referred to it as the *heitzraum*, or boiler room, but what it heated at one time we did not know.

On one side of the barrack the terrain rose steeply. Halfway up the hill, I could see an old wooden door recessed into the ground that led to a bunker. The bunker was off-limits to all of us children, and in the seven years we lived there, I don't think any adult opened the door. I often wondered how deep the bunker was and how many soldiers and civilians it could house. Also part way up the hill, a natural spring gushed fresh water continuously. Anyone could drink the water, and the family that lived in a small house close to the spring used pipes to siphon some water nearer to their home.

On the opposite side of the barrack ran the railroad tracks. Between the tracks and our building, we had a garden. Past the tracks a short distance was a forest where I spent a lot of time playing. Thick carpets of moss covered the ground between the trees. Friends and I spent many pleasant hours pulling up large chunks of moss and laying them on top of each other to make soft beds to lie on. We swung on the heavy vines that hung from the trees and played hide-and-seek. A road ran through the woods not far in, but since few cars drove by, it was always a marvelous surprise to see them. Past the woods and farmland ran the Enns River just far enough away that we could not see it.

We often walked when we had to go to Garsten, the town where we shopped and went to school and church, which was almost three miles because of the winding road. We could make the trip whenever we needed to rather than early in the morning or late in the afternoon when the train ran. We normally took a path across the hills instead of the road. The woods and meadows along the way were fun. We saw beautiful flowers, hunted mushrooms, and picked wild strawberries and raspberries when they were in season. Fruit trees were in abundance, and we picked up many apples and pears that had fallen to the ground.

The natural food we found supplemented our meager diet. We could afford meat only once a week on Sundays, and sometimes not even then. For breakfast, we usually ate dry, dark, homemade bread soaked in a diluted milk mixture or cornmeal. Supper consisted of vegetable soup and bread followed by potatoes, rice, or noodles fixed in a variety of ways. The summer was better since we had garden lettuce, carrots, and other vegetables. My sisters and I also picked dandelion leaves for salad. A special time for the whole family came in late fall when we butchered a hog, smoked some of the meat, made sausages, and rendered lard. Other than butchering a rabbit now and then, the meat was served sparingly to make it last many months.

Daily Chores

We girls were expected to do our share of work and keep a neat home. One of Mother's favorite comments was "Just because we are poor does not mean we have to be dirty." Scrubbing the wood kitchen floor was my oldest sister's weekly chore, but I had jobs too. Daily chores included filling the woodbin, carrying water into the kitchen or emptying the slop bucket, picking grass for the rabbits, or weeding the garden. I often walked to a nearby farmer in the afternoon around milking time to bring home a liter of milk for our breakfast. As the milk sat overnight, the cream rose to the top, which Mother scooped off and saved to make butter.

The daily trips were rather fun since I had the opportunity to see the farmhouse and talk to the farmwife more than I would have otherwise. The setup of Austrian farmsteads was different than the ones in Voćin. The farm buildings were connected to each other around a central courtyard. Living quarters were along one side of the square. Barns for horses, cows, and pigs and chicken coops formed the other sides with wide gates to accommodate movement. Chicken and geese ran around loose and fed on grain strewn on the ground. Milking cows and gathering eggs were daily chores. When the barns needed cleaning, the manure was dumped on a big pile in the courtyard and used as fertilizer in fields and gardens.

We washed our clothes on a washboard. First, we heated the water on the stove and transferred it to a large washtub. Then, using lye soap, we rubbed the clothes against the washboard to remove dirt and stains, rinsed them, and hung them on a clothesline. Sheets, pillowcases, and other white items were boiled on the stove to clean and disinfect them. It took at least two people to wring out water from the sheets by folding the sheets in half and twisting from opposite ends. Not surprisingly, the washtub also became our bathtub.

Mother and Grandmother made the lye soap we used. It was a labor-intensive process but cheap. The basic ingredients are fat, lye, and water. The fat can be the drippings from any kind of fried meat or it can be tallow, the fat from cattle, sheep, or horses. Because lard from hogs is better for frying and baking, tallow is used to make soap, candles, and lubricants. Since we usually did not have tallow, Mother saved drippings or used the lard we had rendered at the time we butchered a hog. The drippings, however, had to be purified to remove meat particles and other impurities. Mother combined the drippings with water and boiled them for an hour or so. After removing the mixture from heat, she added cold water. The foreign substances sank to the bottom, and the clean fat rose to the top. When the fat was cooled and hardened, she skimmed it off and it was ready to use.

I don't know if we could not afford to buy lye or if it simply was not available for purchase, but we had to find another source. Lye is a caustic substance extremely high in sodium commonly made from ash, and we certainly had plenty of that. When it was time to make soap, Mother collected ash from our kitchen stove and stored it until she had enough. She then poured hot water over the ash and let it sit over night. The next day, she removed the ash particles that had floated to the top and strained the rest of the lye water into a clean container. Lye combined with fat becomes soap that is very effective in cleaning dirt and grease. Because lye is caustic and can create extremely violent and volatile chemical reactions, my sisters and I probably did not help Mother with this chore.

I learned to knit and crochet when I was in first or second grade. I still have a doily I crocheted at that time that reminds me of so many things when I look at it. I also darned socks, not only my own but also my dad's, no matter how big the holes. To make darning easier, we had a wooden object shaped like a mushroom with a sturdy handle. We pushed it into the sock, stretched the material over it snugly, and stitched.

"Mushroom" for darning socks

LIKE A HAYSTACK

Sometimes Dad did not have socks, so he wrapped his feet in rags to keep from developing blisters. One can hardly imagine the smell after he had used the same rags for several days without washing them. That happened when he had to be gone two or three days for his job at the lumberyard in Steyr. He was part of the crew that drove a truck and log hauler into the forests, felled trees, and brought back whole trunks to be sawed into boards.

But Dad had a sense of humor. When he removed his boots and unwrapped his feet at the end of the day, he invited us girls to come get a whiff of the wonderful aroma. Of course, we just made faces and backed off when he held up the rags. Fathers (and men in general) in those days did not do housework, and that included caring for their own shoes and boots. Dad's boots got very dirty, and I often had to clean and polish them for the next day. I can't speak for my sisters, but many years later, after I got married, I assumed cleaning my husband's shoes was just a matter of course. It seems silly now to say that I was surprised when he did not expect nor want that. I guess I had been well indoctrinated about a woman's role and responsibilities.

In the summer, my sisters and I went barefoot most of the time and saved our shoes for school and church. Mom and Dad often reminded us to take them off. Theresa especially was told, "Remember, your two sisters will have to wear them." We walked barefoot so much on dirt and gravel roads that the soles of our feet became very tough and almost insensitive.

Some women in the barrack who were seamstresses made our dresses and skirts. Of course, I wore many hand-me-downs from my sisters. We wore heavy knit stockings above the knees and bloomers to keep warm. The bloomers often peeped out from under our skirts, and other children noticed and made fun.

When the grass grew long around the garden and the barracks, Grandpa cut it with a scythe. After it dried, we girls picked it up and stored it in a shed to feed the rabbits in the winter. We also worked in the fields along with our parents and grandparents to harvest potatoes. The farmers used horses and implements to turn up the rows, but workers picked up the potatoes by hand, and we often helped. I also remember harvesting wheat. Farmhands cut the wheat stalks with sickles and laid them in long rows. Others followed, picked up armloads of wheat, and tied the stalks into bundles, or sheaves, using a few wheat stems twisted together and wrapped around the sheaves. I tried to tie a sheave, and Dad or Mom helped me with one or two, but I was not strong enough, so I just picked up the straw for others. The sheaves were left to dry and then threshed.

Besides harvesting potatoes and wheat, I remember men haying. After mowing the pastures, the men raked the grass into long rows, which they turned to dry a day or two later. Then the hay was picked up with pitchforks and hung on wood stakes to keep it from developing mold. The stakes had several arms sticking out from a central post to hold the hay in place.

In retrospect, I realize that a haystack holds deep significance for me. Layer upon layer of hay makes up a stack. It is not the work of one; many workers contribute to its formation like the people and events that shape our lives. A well-formed stack with a strong foundation withholds wind and rain. While the outside looks weathered and in poor condition, the layers underneath survive almost unchanged for a long time.

I think my life is like a haystack. What is evident at the surface might mislead an observer about the real me. I have to be uncovered slowly, layer by layer, to reveal the inner strength and faith that have helped me survive much wind and rain.

Holiday Celebrations

Old Saint Nick and the Devil

In Austria, in the mid-1940s and early 1950s, one day in particular brought hope and fear into children's hearts—December 6, the Feast of Saint Nicholas.

Late in the afternoon as dusk set in, children anxiously anticipated the coming of Saint Nicholas and his companion. A jingling of chains announced their arrival, and our hearts began to thump. We peeked down the long hallway and watched their progress as each family came out to greet them. Saint Nicholas was tall and stately, dressed in long, flowing robes and a hat like a bishop might wear. As he passed out gifts, he patted the children on their heads and praised them for being good.

However, Saint Nicholas was accompanied by the devil, called Krampus. He was dressed in black, and his face was smudged with coal dust. His long tail and pointed ears made him look fearsome. He carried a sack of coal and a chain that rattled as he dragged it along behind him. He was on the lookout for naughty children to whom he gave chunks of coal or whom he scolded. Sometimes he picked up a child, put him or her under his arm, and walked off. The child screamed with fear until the devil let him go.

After Saint Nicholas and the devil had visited everyone and left, families settled in for a quiet evening, and the children, no doubt, promised themselves to be especially good for Christmas.

Christmas

Christmas Past

How did you decorate your Christmas trees?
With baubles, bangles, beads?
Purchased snowflakes, tinsel, angel hair?
Dense with lights, gaudy, glitzy—a grand affair?

Not so for me.

Evenings with family at the kitchen table
Making gifts for the tree, as we were able.
Handmade snowflakes, apples tied with string,
These were two of my favorite things

Walnuts hung in fragile paper baskets
Dozens on an imperfect tree nicely masked it.

Treetop angel made by the best among us
Completed our work and made us joyous.

Small candles in metal clip-on holders
Lit the dark room for a few hours.
Crude stand hid by simple sheet
Covered by gifts sparse but sweet.

These are my precious memories.

Preparations for Christmas in my family were simple and started just a few days before Christmas Eve. Dad or Grandpa would cut down a tree from a nearby forest and set it up in the bedroom. We then decorated the tree with paper cutouts like stars and snowflakes and three-dimensional baskets that Mother taught us girls how to make. If we had apples in storage that were usable, we hung them with string tied to the stems. Finally, we attached real candles in metal holders and lit them every evening for a short time. The tree stayed fresh in the cold, unheated bedroom until January 6, the Feast of the Three Kings, or Epiphany.

After supper on Christmas Eve was quiet family time. First, we opened whatever gifts there were. I think I had only one doll throughout my childhood years, but I don't remember even that very clearly. Afterward, we spent the evening playing games with walnuts and hazelnuts. Each person got two or three walnuts and six or eight hazelnuts. The game with the walnuts was called "ćuću-bert" (choo-choo-bert). The flat end of the nut we called ćuću, and the pointed end we called bert. Mom or Dad started the game by holding a walnut in one fist so no one could see it and asking someone, "Ćuću or bert?" The other person had to guess which end of the nut pointed upward. If the person answered correctly, the person got the nut to keep, and then it was that person's turn to ask someone else the same thing. If the person guessed wrong, he or she had to give a nut to the questioner, and that person would continue to ask others.

The game with the hazelnuts was called "cipar-nepar," or even-odd. Because hazelnuts are small, even I at age six could hold several in my fist. The goal was to ask another person if I had an odd or even number of nuts in my hand. If the person was right, I had to give him or her a nut; if the person was wrong, I got one. At the end of the playing time, the person with the most nuts was the winner.

After that, we often attended midnight Mass.

On Christmas morning, we went to Mass if we had not gone the evening before, and then we ate a late breakfast, which usually consisted of a meat dish made with pork hocks that we called sulz. In the afternoon, we popped popcorn or roasted chestnuts and enjoyed the warmth of the woodstove late into the evening.

Easter

Easter holiday was a big deal when I was a child. It was one of the biggest celebrations in the liturgical year and focused on Christ's resurrection and the arrival of spring. We took more care than normal to dress appropriately for church, and if my sisters and I were given new dresses during the year, this was usually the time. Since I was the youngest girl, I wore my sisters' hand-me-downs, but occasionally I got a new dress too.

Easter Saturday was filled with activity. While Mother began preparations for Easter dinner, we girls cleaned and put everything in order. The most important job was to prepare for the coming of the Easter rabbit. Each of us had her own nest made of grass. We picked new shoots of grass wherever we could find them. When spring came early, or when Easter came late, picking enough grass was easy, but other years the grass simply had not sprouted, so we were challenged to find enough shoots here and there to form a skimpy nest. Each of us chose a spot in the kitchen and carefully molded the soft, rounded nests to hold the Easter gifts.

Like all children, we awoke Easter morning with great hope and anticipation, but our presents were always meager. Once I asked my sisters what we actually found in our nests, but not one of us could remember. Perhaps an orange or a piece of candy. I can only imagine how bad Mom and Dad must have felt to disappoint us so often because they had nothing to give.

Escargot and Other Strange Delicacies

Have you ever eaten escargot? Escargot is a fancy French name for a common mollusk, the snail. Thousands of varieties of snails can be found in a wide range of environments, including ditches, deserts, and the depths of the sea. The larger varieties of land snails make better eating and are found in greater numbers in Europe than in the United States.

Snails provide a good source of protein, and my family ate them frequently. We simply looked for them in the low spots along railroad tracks and other areas. Grandfather threw them into dying wood embers to roast, and he knew just how to clean them. No wonder I do not have an awed view of escargot. I do admit, however, that one has to become accustomed to its salty flavor and the combination of chewy and soft parts.

We ate many natural products found in our environment. We picked the blossoms and leaves from linden trees to make tea. We did the same with chamomile flowers. Chamomile tea is known for its calming properties, so mothers often gave sick children chamomile as a natural remedy. We picked dandelion leaves for salads and used the blossoms of elderberry bushes to dip into batter and fry like pancakes. We hunted mushrooms and knew how to distinguish between the safe and poisonous ones. We picked domesticated and wild gooseberries, currants, hazelnuts, and edible chestnuts. We grew poppies and used the poppy seeds to make all kinds of pastries.

We became familiar with a variety of plants and could recognize them in the wild. For example, chestnuts, walnuts, and hazelnuts grow on trees, but hazelnuts grow the shortest and produce the best when

LIKE A HAYSTACK

pruned yearly to bush height. It was common to find hazelnut bushes growing among other bushes while looking for wild raspberries or gooseberries. They blended in, so we children did not know that they were considered trees.

Almost every spring or summer, we bought a pig and raised it. Since we did not have a barn, and the pig could not be allowed to roam freely, we kept it inside a shed that Dad had built. Mother fed it every day whatever cooked grains and leftovers we had. We wanted the pig as fat as possible. By late summer or early fall, the pig was so heavy it could not walk or even stand up. Mother actually had to hand feed it.

When the weather turned cold, it was time to slaughter the hog. We considered ourselves lucky if the first snowfall of the season happened on the day we had chosen. We used every part of the pig, even those most people might throw away. As the pig was butchered, Mother caught the blood in a big pan, stirring briskly and continuously until it cooled. Once it did, it did not coagulate, and we used some of it to make blood sausage.

We rinsed pig intestines over and over and filled them with the ground meat using a special grinder attachment. After stuffing the sausages, we cooked them in a big pot. In the same pot, we cooked bones and cut off every last scrap of meat to use in some way. The broth made an excellent soup base. We added pork brains to scrambled eggs for a nutritious meal. We rendered the fat to make lard. To preserve the meat for use during the entire winter, we put it into big vats covered with lard. Rendering the fat produced brown, crusty, tasty remains called crackling. We ate much more pork than beef, but we sometimes bought tripe, which is the rubbery lining of the stomach of cattle. We simmered the tripe in water for a long time to make it tender. Then Mother cut it into pieces, dredged the pieces in eggs and flour, and fried them in oil or lard until they were crispy brown and tasty.

We ate everything. We gnawed bones clean, ate the gristle, and even broke the bones to suck out the tasty marrow, especially with chicken bones. Mother's command always was "Do not throw away anything edible." She kept an observant eye on my sisters and me whenever we peeled vegetables or fruit. "Cut off only the very tip or stem end, not an inch or more. What is the point of wasting good food? Cut the thinnest layer possible off an apple or potato. Eat an apple all the way to the core; get every bit. If you can't do that, don't take one." I certainly learned how to use a paring knife, and I challenged myself to see how thin and long my strips of paring could be.

Our food was simple and mostly homegrown but good. Besides limited portions, there are some basic differences between cooking then and now. We used lard for just about everything, mainly because it was all we had, but lard has few good substitutes when it comes to frying and baking. It adds such wonderful flavor and aroma to food. Smear a bit of the residue from crackling on a piece of heavy white or dark bread, and you will savor every bite.

Another difference is in the sauces we made. Today, cooks make a lot of white sauce, a thickening made with butter, flour, and milk. We made rue by browning flour in lard or oil until it was dark brown. Toward the end of the browning process, we added chopped onions or garlic and then water for a thick or thin consistency, depending on its use. The brown mixture added a deep, full-bodied flavor to dishes like tomato soup or cabbage rolls. Soups were a staple in our home. Hardly a day went by without some kind of soup. It was nutritious, filling, and satisfying.

I admit we tired of heavy wheat and rye bread, especially when they were days or weeks old. Mother baked, but we also bought bread from farmers' wives who baked many loaves at a time in large brick ovens. I often watched in amazement as the wife of a local farmer used a wood paddle with a long handle to reach deep into the oven to pull out large loaves. She baked perhaps a dozen loaves at a time to feed her family and hired hands for several weeks. The loaves kept well without molding, but they became very hard and dry by the next baking day. Then the only way to eat the bread was to soak it in coffee or soup. When we needed bread, we were fortunate to buy some from a fresh batch.

The sweet corn and popcorn we grew were allowed to ripen until the kernels were dry. After harvesting the ears, we stored them in a cool place, usually the space above the rafters in the building where we lived. When we wanted to eat some, we shelled the ears by hand. The sweet corn had to be soaked for a long time, usually overnight, and then cooked slowly. Of course, it was not very sweet, but it was good and nutritious. For the popcorn, Dad made a wood-frame box with a wire-mesh bottom. We put the box with popcorn on our preheated stove and shook it continuously until the corn was popped.

Other garden produce did not store so easily. When we had lots of cabbage, we made sauerkraut. The cabbage was sliced thin, mixed with salt, and put into a crock of some kind. A board with a rock or other weight was put on top to keep the cabbage submerged in the brine. In a week or two, bubbles appeared around the edges of the board, and we knew the cabbage was fermenting. Occasionally, Mother used a wet cloth to skim off the brownish residue that accumulated. After two months or so, the cabbage was ready to use, and it kept well for months.

Grandparents

Otata and Omama Wahl (Grandpa and Grandma, mother's parents)

Other than introducing them at the beginning of my story, I have not said much about Otata Franz and Omama Marija Wahl. It goes without saying that whenever I refer to Dad and Mom and our activities, Otata and Omama were included.

Grandpa was a tall, handsome, strong man and very good to his grandchildren. Because Theresa was the oldest grandchild, she went with him often to hunt mushrooms and berries and walk to Garsten. She enjoyed being with him. I missed out on those trips because I was too little, but I remember the fun of being dandled on his knee.

Grandma was short and squat and wore a scarf on her head all the time. She folded the scarf low over her forehead and around her face. Her hair was always combed back and rolled into a bun.

In the evening, she exchanged her daytime scarf for one she wore to bed; she was never without one, even though she had nice hair. While many older women wore scarves, I knew of no other woman who wore one to bed.

Grandma's clothing consisted of long skirts, aprons, and long-sleeved blouses. She also was stoop shouldered. She had hurt her back picking up heavy loads of wood when she was a young mother and farm wife.

Theresa told me a sad story, but she knew only minimal facts. Grandpa and Grandma had a son. However, before the baby was weaned, Grandma had to be gone for some time and asked a neighbor woman to take care of the boy. When the baby needed to be fed, the woman gave it regular cow's milk. The baby reacted to the milk and died.

Grandma Marija & Grandpa Franz Wahl outside their house in Lahrndorf

LIKE A HAYSTACK

Đedo and Bakica Grgurić (Grandpa and Grandma, Dad's parents)

I have not said anything about my father's family, and I truly regret to say that neither my sisters nor I know much. My dad's parents were Nikola and Alojzia Grgurić. They lived in Osijek, about eighty-eight kilometers, or fifty-five miles, from Voćin. We could not walk that far, and it was not easy to travel that distance with horse and wagon, so we simply did not see them.

Grandfather Nikola was a forest ranger. Grandmother was most certainly a hardworking mother of four. Dad had two brothers, Andrija (Andrew) and Jożo (Joseph), and a sister, Adela. Grandpa and the brothers were killed during World War II. Adela married a man by the name of Branko Aćić, but they had no children. Both survived the war, and Dad wrote to them and his mother regularly. The only time I remember seeing Grandma Alojzija was when she visited us in Austria shortly before we left for America. Like Grandma Marija, she wore a scarf every day.

Grandma Alojzia Grguric, Dad's mother

Garsten

Benedictine Church and monastery in Garsten

GARSTEN IS THE TOWN WHERE my sisters and I went to school, where our family attended church, and where my grandparents were buried. I am fascinated by its ancient beginnings.

The earliest documentation for the town dates back as far as 990 AD. A monastery was founded there in 1089 AD. More than five hundred years later, in the 1600s, the monastery was rebuilt in Baroque style, ornate and complex. Around 1625, it became a Benedictine monastery and functioned as such for more than two hundred years. It was the religious, spiritual, and cultural center of the region throughout its history. Local people attended services at the church on Sundays and holy days.

At some point, perhaps around the mid-1800s, the monastery was converted to a prison. The church, however, continued to serve as a parish church. My family frequently walked by the church and prison, and not knowing the history of the place, we often wondered why the buildings were attached to each other. The prison housed men sentenced to life, and several times we observed prisoners chained together being escorted out through the large gates.

The territorial subdivisions of Austria are important to understand. The Republic of Austria, with its capital Vienna, is a federation of nine autonomous provinces, or states. Each state is divided into districts, or counties (*bezirk*). Garsten is located in the state of Upper Austria (Oberösterreich) in the district of Steyr-Land.

Garsten today is a town of about six thousand residents located along the Enns River. It is a lovely town with many amenities. Mountain climbing, hiking, and skiing are common activities, and a ski resort is less than ten miles away. According to census data, the population increased by fewer than one thousand residents between 1980 and 2010, so to put its population in 1950 at around five thousand is realistic.

The Enns River, about 158 miles long, is a tributary of the Danube and is the fifth largest river in Austria. It begins in the state of Salzburg and travels east-northeast until it empties into the Danube River. Since it is a white-water river with many rapids and frothy, challenging waves, it is one of the most popular rafting destinations in the world. The speed of the river and its steep falls make it ideal for the many power plants that have been built along it, one of which is located close to Garsten. The river is also an important link between the towns of Garsten, Steyr, and Enns, towns where we went to school, worked, or visited.

School in Garsten

Train station in Garsten where we waited for hours to ride home

When my sisters and I attended school in Garsten, we either walked the four kilometers (close to three miles) or took the train. The train left the Lahrndorf station around 6:30 a.m., so we had to get up early and walk three-fourths of a mile to get there on time. Often we had to stand up inside the car all the way to town or stand on a crowded platform between the cars.

We disembarked at the Garsten station and walked a few blocks to school. Because we were too early, the school was not open, and we waited outside at least half an hour until the janitor arrived. In the winter, the building was extremely cold. Each classroom had a coal stove that the janitor had to stoke and light. It took a long time for the warmth to bring relief to our numb hands and feet.

Perhaps it is not necessary to mention that Austrians speak German. I have known people who were not aware that the Austrian Empire was one of the world's largest empires in the 1800s and the largest country in the German Confederation. It eventually became part of the Austria-Hungarian Empire. The official German language is High German, or

Hochdeutsch, but it has many dialects—between 50 and 250, depending on one's definition of dialect. Even if one knows high-German well, one can suddenly encounter a person whom one cannot understand.

The official version is used in business, tourist situations, and usually in schools and is the version I normally hear on the radio or TV programs. My sisters and I spoke High German at school and switched to a low-German dialect as soon as we arrived home. I can attest to the fact that I can no longer communicate in the dialect with anyone from the area in which we lived. It is easy to forget if all one hears is High German.

I remember little of the first four years of school, perhaps because I was still learning the German language. Also, since I was a foreigner, other children did not associate with me much. Even the teachers were not very friendly. On several occasions, the teacher carried a box into the classroom and told us it was a CARE package from America. None of us children knew what that meant for years, but we were thrilled when she pulled out a variety of items. CARE, the Cooperative for American Remittances to Europe, initiated a program in 1945 to send food relief to Europe where large numbers of people were at risk of starvation after the war. The packages came from surplus supplies originally meant to feed American soldiers. They contained what people needed most: meat, cheese, fruit and vegetables, sugar and coffee, butter, condensed milk, cornflakes, chewing gum, and other items.

After opening the package, the teacher distributed items to whomever she wished. While she tried to make sure every student received something, I was often passed over. Other students received two or three items before I was given one that no one else wanted. Once I received a dental hygiene kit: a toothbrush and container of tooth powder. I tried using the powder, but it was inconvenient and completely alien to me since I had never brushed my teeth before.

I understand the challenges Austrians faced. They suffered much because of Hitler's war, and having to deal with displaced persons, or DPs as we were referred to, added to their hardship. Millions of people who had fled their countries had to be repatriated. By the end of 1945, over six million refugees were sent back to their countries of origin. In 1946, the United Nations created the International Refugee Organization (IRO) to help with the refugee problem. Eighteen countries became members of IRO and agreed to accept refugees. Many who were not repatriated simply had to be absorbed into the local society. Under the circumstances, I think the Austrians did the best they could.

School, of course, was fun as well. The Austrian school system incorporated class trips into the curriculum even for the lower-grade students. On special holidays, we were driven into the hills or certain places of interest and walked and observed whatever the teachers pointed out. One of our trips was to Schoberstein, one of the most beautiful peaks of the Alps, located in Upper Austria. We became familiar with alpine flowers, such as edelweiss and enzian, and love of forests and hills entered our souls and became a part of us forever. The songs of the peasants were fun and lively, and we especially liked to listen to yodeling, a type of song in which the voice fluctuates quickly from high to low. My sisters and I learned to do simple yodels to several songs. Everybody did it.

On the playground, besides running and skipping rope, we played a game I will never forget. To understand it, I need to provide a little background information.

Chimney sweeps, or *rauchfangkehrer* (smokestack cleaners), were a common sight in Austria. These "men in black," carrying brushes with long, coiled metal handles hung over their shoulders, went to houses and businesses to clean chimneys and fireplaces that had thick buildup of soot on the inside. Doing this several times a year prevented the soot from clogging chimneys or catching on fire. While there are not as many chimney sweeps today, both men and women still earn their livelihood doing this kind of work.

For reasons I do not understand, these men became romantic figures over the half century or more of their existence. At school, we children often played a game that involved a chimney sweep and a young girl. The game went like this. A group of boys and girls, holding hands, formed a large circle. Three of them were chosen to play the roles of chimney sweep, a young, dark-brown girl, and the girl's father. The girl stood inside the circle, the chimney sweep stood outside, and the father was part of the circle. The rest of the children sang a song while the characters acted it out and sang their parts.

Rauchfangkehrer ging spazieren...
The chimney sweep goes for a walk around the circle.

Kam er an ein schönes Haus...
He comes to a house—two children stand side by side with their arms lifted high to form a V-shape. The dark-brown (black-brown) girl in the center of the circle looks out this "window" as the chimney sweep approaches. The song then goes as follows:

Mädel, kannst du mit mir gehen?
"Mädel (girl), can you go with me?" the chimney sweep sings.

Muss ich erst den Vater fragen.
"I have to ask my father first," she replies and walks toward the father.

Vater, kann ich mit ihm gehen?
"Father, may I go with him?" she begs sweetly.

Nein, mein Kind, das darfst du night.
"No, my child, you may not," the father answers.

Laufen Sie zum Tor hinaus
They run out the door.

Kamen Sie nach Afrika
They arrive in Africa.

Kaufen Sie ein Zwillingspaar
They buy a pair of black children.

Never having seen an African-American person before, I did not understand for years the "dark-brown girl" connotation. Because a chimney sweep's face and hands were usually covered with soot, they would have made a likely pair. Can you imagine children being allowed to sing such a song nowadays? I came to learn that this song had several versions, and one ending simply refers to a wedding celebration after the couple runs away.

Even though I had contact with children at school, I knew very little about their personal lives. Only once did I have a glimpse into the life of one student, Lori. Away from school, we played together mainly because we lived near each other and there were no other girls our age. Over time, though, we became friends, but the social status of our families kept us from developing a close friendship.

Lori lived in a lovely large two-story house located next to the train station since her father was the stationmaster. I was invited inside her house only once that I remember. I felt uncomfortable and awkward because Lori's life and home were so different from mine. I was astonished to see large, well-furnished rooms. The living room especially surprised me since in the middle of it sat a grand piano. I had never seen one before, so I did not know that it was a "grand" piano. I also had never heard one played before. It was so beautiful; I just stared. All I knew was that Lori took piano lessons every week in the town of Steyr about six miles away. She sometimes invited me to walk to Steyr with her, and I waited outside the building while she had her lesson.

Because of her father's job, the family was well off. Lori wore nice clothes to school and had plenty of food to eat even if they could not buy everything they might have wanted. I do not know if Lori's family was typical; I just noticed its contrast to mine. When I moved to America during fourth grade, Lori and I lost touch. I often wonder how her life turned out.

National Holidays

Garsten, like every town in Austria, celebrated important national holidays, one of which was May 1, or Labor Day. It was a day to drink and dance and celebrate not only Labor Day but also spring.

Carnival rides were set up in town. I enjoyed the swing ride, or *ringlspiel*, the most. It consisted of a tall center post with a large wheel mounted horizontally at the top. Fifteen to twenty swings hung on ropes from the wheel. The ride started to spin slowly and then picked up speed as the swings moved out and skyward, higher and higher into the blue. The sensation was scary yet exhilarating. I did not see a ride similar to this in America for many years. I eventually rode one, but it was not as tall or exciting as the ones I remember. The shorter versions found at carnivals today simply do not compare.

In addition to the carnival rides, a Maypole up to forty-five feet tall was erected in the town square and decorated with flowers and long ribbons attached at the top. Dancers, usually young girls, gathered around the pole in a circle. Each dancer held one of the ribbons and kept it taut while they performed a weaving routine. Half the girls walked in one direction and the rest in the opposite direction.

About half of the pole from the ground up was smeared with grease or soap. At some point in the afternoon, young men and boys tried their luck at climbing the pole to the top to grab the flowers or pretzels and sausage hanging there and win a prize. It was fun to watch so many boys try and fail until one managed to get past the slippery part, scale to the top, and slip down to the cheers of the crowd.

A boy succeeds in climbing the May Pole.

It was common to see men and boys wear lederhosen. Lederhosen were pants, short or knee-length, made of leather. More durable than fabric pants, they were worn mostly for hard physical labor. Women and girls wore *dirndlkleider*. *Dirndl* refers to a young woman, and *kleid* means dress. The dirndl consisted of a blouse, a full skirt with a bodice, and an apron. What we see nowadays is more for show and dress up than for work.

Lederhosen and Dirndlkleid: Short leather pants for boys and skirt, blouse, and apron for girls

I mentioned that my grandparents are buried in the cemetery next to the church. The cemetery is different from what we normally see in America but is common in Austria. The graves are narrow, and the dirt is built up into mounds above each one and planted with flowers and shrubs. Some are simple, and others are quite elaborate. The paths between individual plots are barely wide enough to walk so as to conserve on space. The entire effect of the cemetery, however, is quite lovely.

Steyr and Enns

In the course of writing my story and researching towns close to Garsten that my family frequented, I have been fascinated by the history not only of the area as a whole but of Steyr and Enns as well.

The county seat of Steyr-Land was, and still is, the town of Steyr, several miles past Garsten. It was the town where my father and grandfather worked and where my friend Lori took piano lessons. Theresa often walked there to visit Grandmother when she was in the hospital. Information about the town is easy to find since it is a favorite place to visit. It celebrated its one-thousand-year anniversary in 1980.

Huddled at the foot of a cliff at the junction of the Steyr and Enns rivers, Steyr enjoys the reputation of being one of the prettiest cities in Oberösterreich (Upper Austria). Some consider it a rival of Vienna. Its beautiful downtown district is a blend of Gothic, Renaissance, and Baroque architecture. The town grew wealthy from Austria's iron industry and firearms manufacturing, and it still thrives on that legacy. It is the home to leading international groups in mechanical engineering and the metal industry. The town is dotted with historic fortifications, ancient fountains, and dozens of bridges and footbridges. One of the most well known of these is the Zwischenbrücke, a large bridge across the Enns River close to where another bridge comes across the Steyr River.

Another twelve miles northeast of Steyr is the town of Enns, possibly the oldest town in Austria. The first settlement dates back four thousand years. It was incorporated into the Roman Empire and designated a Roman province in 45 AD. It is located at the mouth of the Enns River where it joins the Danube, just sixteen miles from Linz, the capital of Upper Austria.

The Old World for those of us with European roots is the site of two of the world's most horrific wars, which destroyed countless people, land, and structures. Yet Europe also retains some of the most beautiful buildings and art ever produced. Many buildings have existed for hundreds of years, even centuries—providing contrast to buildings that do not survive more than 150 years or are considered obsolete in even fewer years.

The more I come to know about this part of Austria, the more in awe I am of its history, natural beauty, and many riches. I am also surprised by the proximity of the towns that I mentioned. Since we traveled mostly on foot and occasionally by train, these places seemed so far apart and were unfamiliar to me.

Part II
A NEW LAND

The Trip to America

Dad achieved his goal of providing a better life for his family in February 1952 after persistent effort. Theresa in her account explained the reasons for the protracted process of leaving Austria, and perhaps, in the end, we were fortunate. At age nine, I had no idea what was happening; I simply followed my parents' lead. Nothing was explained to me in terms I could understand.

The three weeks at sea from Bremerhaven, Germany, to New Orleans are difficult to describe. My father seemed to handle the ocean voyage fairly well, but my mother was seasick from the first day to the last. Although my sisters and I had bouts of seasickness, we felt well enough to explore the ship and enjoy the fresh air on deck. Watching whales glide by in the distance and seeing schools of flying fish never ceased to amaze me.

The changes in the ocean were equally amazing. One day, the water was smooth and glossy; the next day, huge, dark waves crashed against the ship. The ship heaved and sank in endless cycles, making seasickness much worse. One day the storm was so intense and the waves so high and rough that the bow of the ship dipped low, scooped up water, and sprayed the deck when it came up. Everyone on deck had to hold tightly to ropes to avoid being tossed around or swept overboard.

The most surprising event I witnessed was a burial at sea. All I remember is a wood casket placed on a long board that jutted across the railing over the water. The casket was pushed to the end until it slid off.

In the hold of the ship, the men and boys were separated from the women and girls. Mother and we girls were assigned to a room filled with rows of bunk beds stacked at least three high. I had to take an upper berth close to the ceiling, so I could not sit up in bed. I either had to lie down or be on the floor. I walked the narrow hallways to the deck or the mess hall since there was nothing else to do.

Eating was always an experience. The food was served cafeteria style, and we took the trays to the tables on unsteady feet as the ship pitched and rolled. I was always concerned that the dishes would slide off the table. One day at a meal we were given whole grapefruit. Never having had them before, we did not eat them right away but took them with us. Later, my sisters and I tried to peel them as we would oranges, but, of course, they did not peel easily nor separate into sections. When we tasted them, we were surprised and disappointed at the bitter taste. We could not eat them and threw them away. A day or two later, I happened to notice a man in the mess hall eating a grapefruit, and I watched him in amazement. He did not peel it but cut it, sprinkled sugar on the pieces, and seemed to relish every bite. It was years before I learned to do the same.

We docked at the Port of New Orleans on February 19, 1952. My only memory after disembarking is standing in a throng of people waiting to be told what to do and where to go. To this day, I marvel at those people whose job it was to keep families together and make sure they were herded in the right direction, as we numbered in the thousands. We were put on a train to Chicago where we transferred to go to Iowa. The trip took three days.

Ossian, Iowa

February–June 1952

WE WERE MET AT THE train depot, I do not know where, by a farmer, Mr. S., who was our sponsor. Many people like Mr. S. housed and provided jobs for immigrants like us. In return, the immigrants were expected to work for the host for some time to repay his monetary investment. Dad became his hired man.

We rode in Mr. S.'s car to his farm not far from Ossian, Iowa. It was night when we arrived, and we looked forward to our journey's end. However, our "homecoming" was a huge disappointment. We walked into a large kitchen and saw the sink, countertops, and table overflowing with dirty dishes, pots, and pans. It was awful. We were ushered upstairs to our bedrooms. My sisters and I shared one room.

The next morning, after breakfast, Dad went outside with the farmer. We women were not told what to do, but of course, we had few options. The first order of the day was to clean the kitchen. We found out that Mr. S. was divorced, but even that did not entirely explain the condition in which he lived. In the course of the next few weeks, Mother and we girls cleaned the entire house and brought some routine and order into our lives. Mother helped with farm chores as well.

From February until the end of the school year, my sisters and I attended the Catholic school in Ossian. The teachers decided it would be best to keep Rosi and me together and put us in grade four, which was right for me but not for her. Theresa was placed into grade eight even though she was beyond that. It really did not matter; the teachers simply tried to do their best for us. However, Rosi and I stayed in the same grade for the rest of our elementary grades.

My memories are few and indistinct, but I remember one in particular. I stood at the edge of the playground during lunch recess and simply observed the children playing tag or skipping rope. After some time, a girl my age walked over to me and handed me a part of her lunch, a banana. Awkwardly, I thanked her in words she could not understand and wondered what to do with the piece of fruit I had never eaten before. I watched the other children and carefully peeled it. Its sweetness and soft, smooth texture appealed to me, and I was grateful for her kindness.

I often think of that girl whose name is lost in my memory. Of all the children on the playground, she was the one who noticed a lonely girl and responded. Perhaps she had a special gift, a sensitivity that allowed her to see my need. For a brief moment, she bridged our differences and gave me hope. I will never forget her. Her friendship touched me in a way she could not have anticipated. Now, years later, no incident from my early days in America is as clear in my mind as the time I received that banana. For three or four months, she and other girls included me in their games, and I slowly adapted to my new school. But my family moved unexpectedly to another part of the state during the summer, and I did not see them again.

My parents were hardworking people who gave more than was expected of them. Before too long, Dad recognized that he and Mother were being taken advantage of. After three months of not receiving their promised wages, Dad decided to move the family.

We had become acquainted with a family of German heritage with whom Mom and Dad could speak a little German. This was a blessing since we knew no English. This man knew of a farmer near Marble Rock, Iowa, who needed help, and he drove Dad to meet with Peter Marzen and his wife, Lucille. Mr. Marzen, however, had already hired someone just days prior to Dad's visit. Fortunately, though, Mr. Marzen's brother-in-law, Matt Heinz, needed a worker and was willing to hire Dad.

Matt and his wife, Minnie, lived in Charles City but owned land close to Roseville, and we moved into a house they had lived in prior to retiring and moving to town. We left Ossian with fewer than ten dollars in our pockets. Eventually, we met the family whom Mr. Marzen had hired. To our surprise, Marco B. was from Yugoslavia and his wife, Anna, from Germany. We had much in common and became good friends.

Roseville, Iowa

1952–1955

THE DIFFERENCES BETWEEN MR. S. and Mr. Heinz can hardly be described. Mr. Heinz gave Dad an advance on his monthly wages, and he brought us a basket of meat every week with plenty of pork and bacon. For the first time in our lives, we had more than we could eat. Mother took care of the chickens, and we could have as many eggs as we needed. Our thin, undernourished bodies could not get enough. For a while, Dad actually ate a dozen eggs for breakfast along with lots of bacon and bread. After some months (maybe even years), we slowly cut back and ate normal portions.

Mr. Marzen did not forget us, either. After a few days, he loaned us a cow. Mother milked the cow daily, and we had plenty of milk to drink and to make butter and cottage cheese. Since Mr. and Mrs. Marzen had a large family, several of their children were close to my age, so they frequently invited me to their farm to spend time with them. On one such visit, several of us piled into their pickup to go to town. I reached out so far to shut the door that I practically fell out. I grabbed the side of the pickup and smashed my left index finger as I shut the door. Instead of having fun, I had to be taken to the doctor.

The Marzens' generosity, friendship, and understanding helped me transition again to another unfamiliar place. Even though they eventually moved to a farm near Stacyville, Iowa, and we moved to Des Moines, we maintained contact with them over the years and were treated like family whenever we visited.

The house we moved into was an ordinary two-story farmhouse with a nice-sized kitchen, dining room, large living room, and bedroom

LIKE A HAYSTACK

on the ground floor. The living room ceiling had a register in the middle to allow heat to rise to the second floor. A wood-burning stove was situated on the floor directly below the register.

The upstairs had three bedrooms. For the first time in my life, we had room to move around and not get in each other's way. The yard and driveway between the house and outbuildings gave us lots of room to run around as well.

Life on the farm was normal. Dad worked with Mr. Heinz's son, John, who lived a mile or so from us with his wife and two daughters. Dad knew enough about farming that he did not have to learn many new things—except one. Matt or John must have mentioned problems with a skunk, so Dad decided to catch it and get rid of it. However, he was not familiar with skunks and got sprayed. There was not much he or Mother could do to wash the stink off him.

Mother planted a large garden surrounded by a fence to protect it from farm animals. In the spring, Mr. Heinz or John took down a portion of the fence, plowed the garden, and replaced the fence. The nuns from the church in Roseville gave us seeds. In addition to familiar vegetable seeds, they gave us seeds for ground cherries, which were quite unusual. Local farm wives made ground cherry pie or sauce, and Mother made some of that, too, but I don't think most of my family developed a liking for them.

We had a cute little dog named Putzi that someone gave us, and we enjoyed it. It was full of life and liked to be petted. Only once did the dog have too much fun when it jumped to reach clothes on the line and tattered several of them. Needless to say, from then on the clotheslines were propped up with long poles so high the dog could not reach anything.

I did not spend much time with John's two girls who were younger than I. The differences in our customs and daily routine amazed me. The mother maintained a meticulous yard and home, and her care extended to her daughters. They had lovely blond hair that the mother rolled up every morning. They looked so cute in their curly, bouncy hair. My sisters and I had long hair that had never been cut. Mine reached below my waist, and I wore it in pigtails. Eventually it became long enough to sit on. I couldn't imagine having my hair curled every day.

Saint Mary's Church and School

Our house was approximately four miles from the town of Roseville. The town consisted of Saint Mary's Church, the rectory, and another large house. They were situated a short distance from each other on the west side of Highway 14, about eight miles north of the town of Greene. A grocery store and gas station stood across the street.

We were introduced to the priest at Saint Mary's Church in Roseville, Father Kirchhof, and to the nuns shortly after we arrived. The sisters were very kind, and I am sure they invited us to go to school at Saint Mary's. We couldn't, though, because we did not have a car to travel the four miles to town. One of the sisters, probably the music teacher, was especially kind to me. She gave me a small harmonica one day with a thin booklet of songs and showed me how to play it. It was an unusual and unexpected gift, and the songs gave me information about America and its history without my being aware of it. I truly enjoyed learning songs like "Flow Gently, Sweet Afton," "Taps," "Danny Boy," "Oh Suzanna," "Swanee River," and "Old Black Joe." Only years later did I recognize how these songs reflected the influence of Irish immigrants and slavery on American culture.

In the 1950s, there was not as much concern about political correctness as there is now, and we saw nothing wrong in singing and playing any of those songs. We did not consider them disrespectful. They simply spoke of times in the recent history of our new country, times we should not forget. We were ignorant as to how the people about whom we sang would have reacted. I still remember the words to "Old Black Joe," and the gentle melody haunts me to this day.

> Gone are the days when my heart was young and gay.
> Gone are my friends from the cotton fields away.
> Gone from the earth to a better land I know
> I hear their gentle voices calling, "Old Black Joe."
> I'm coming, I'm coming, for my head is bending low.
> I hear their gentle voices calling, "Old Black Joe."

I am surprised how many people close to my age do not know these songs since they were common. In fact, one year at a meeting of the Orchard Legion Auxiliary, I suggested singing "Taps" at a Memorial Day program instead of just listening to recording of it. Not one woman knew that the song has several verses that explain clearly why it is used at funerals of soldiers and on Veterans' Day. I guess I would not know the words and melodies either if it had not been for that kind nun in Roseville.

We attended church every Sunday. After Mass, without fail, we stopped at the gas station and grocery store right across the street from the church. There, we did our weekly grocery shopping. We made few trips to more distant towns like Greene or Marble Rock. If the Roseville market did not have something, we simply made do without it.

I remember a funny incident at the store. Mother asked for something that sounded like "grease" in English. The storeowner showed her butter, lard, oil, and perhaps other things. He and Mother simply did not understand each other. So we went home without "cream of wheat." What a strange name that seemed to us later. At about the same time, Father Kirchhof finally convinced me not to say please when someone said thank you, and that the correct response is "You are welcome." In German, *danke* (thank you) is followed by *bitte* (please). He sounded really irritated one day when I said bitte again, and I finally understood I had to change.

Someone must have given us a ride to church at first, but then Dad bought an old car from Father Kirchhof. It was a clunker. When it did not start by turning the ignition key, Dad used a crank, a crowbar of sorts, inserted it into the crankshaft at the front of the car, and turned with all his might until the engine fired. He had to do this almost every time we went anywhere. Theresa was usually the one who sat behind the wheel and worked the clutch. Sometimes all of us except Dad got out and pushed until the car moved fast enough to start. It was also a two-door, so climbing in and out was inconvenient. Our first experience with a car had its benefits and drawbacks.

MARGARET GRGURIĆ SMOLIK

My family with Father Kirchhof at the farm by Roseville

Mother, Theresa, Rosi, and Margaret on the farm

Margaret and dog Putzi

One-Room School (1952–1954)

IN THE FALL OF 1952, my fifth-grade year, Rosi and I attended the one-room elementary school within walking distance of our house. Theresa did not attend school with us. She was already sixteen years old, so the priest at Saint Mary's church helped her find a job as a nanny and housekeeper for a local family whose mother had health issues and needed help.

There were perhaps fifteen students at school. The teacher grouped us in clusters of two or three grades. When the teacher was finished with one group, she gave the students work to do on their own while she taught the next level. Older children were often asked to work with the younger ones. Teaching all eight grades was typical for a one-room school; that the teacher also had to prepare our lunch was not typical. Students were assigned days, once or twice a week, when they had to take potatoes and other vegetables to the teacher. Before school started, she combined the ingredients, put the pot on the stove, checked it occasionally throughout the morning, and served us a tasty, nutritious soup.

Respect for the teacher and for each other was normal behavior. I do not remember ever being made fun of by other students or left out of games. At recess, we played tag or just stood around waiting for class to resume. At the last minute, we made a quick trip to the outhouse and were ready when the bell rang for us to go inside.

It is true that one learns a language one word at a time. While I do not remember the how and when of every English word I learned, two particular incidents are burned into my memory. Every week, the teacher gave us a new list of twenty to twenty-five spelling words. I had to study especially hard, but I caught on fairly rapidly and learned the meaning and spelling of each word … except one week. During the test on Friday, the teacher pronounced an unfamiliar word, which confused me since I thought I knew every word. Finally, I wrote down what sounded like "tuff." Later, I was surprised to discover that the word on the spelling list was *tough*. The teacher understood my mistake and patiently explained the difference. I have never missed that word since.

Another time that same year, Zita, one of the Marzen girls, and I rode our bicycles on the gravel road close to her farm. I had gotten way ahead of her, and I heard her shout something. Not understanding her, I continued pedaling. She shouted again and again, each time more insistently, until I realized that "wait" meant "stop." So I stopped and waited until she caught up to me. We then continued riding together instead of separately.

Years later, Theresa told me about an embarrassing incident she had experienced. One of the employees at Armstrong Tire Company where she worked was named Richard. Coworkers, naturally, called him Dick. One day, Theresa explained to Dick the meaning of the word *dick* in German: thick, fat, big. Later, a woman who had overheard the conversation told Theresa about another meaning of "dick" in English. The reader can appreciate the humor in combining the two meanings in relation to Dick. Theresa was constantly reminded of it and was embarrassed whenever she saw him. She was glad when, not long after this incident, she left to work for another company.

I learned about American customs in other awkward ways. No one explained to me the purpose or meaning of Valentine's Day. All I understood was that students exchanged cards, and I did not want to be left out. But when Dad took me to the store, I did not know what to look for. After much hesitation and confusion, I picked out cards for all the students. When the clerk told us how much they cost, Dad was really angry. They were simply too expensive. I later learned I could have purchased much cheaper boxes of cards rather than regular greeting cards.

Approximately two years later, my parents somehow found out that people we had known in Yugoslavia lived in Des Moines. We made contact and visited them at their home. After months of deliberation, Mom and Dad decided to move to Des Moines, and the next phase of our lives began.

The Move to Des Moines, Iowa

1955-1964

IN DES MOINES, WE MOVED into a large two-story house owned by John and Mary L. and stayed with them some months. Rosi and I attended Saint Ambrose elementary school until we purchased a house on the south side of Des Moines in a neighborhood known as Little Italy.

Our two-story house was rather small but adequate. The kitchen and dining area were part of one big room. At the end opposite the kitchen was a staircase that led to two bedrooms upstairs. Rosi and I shared a room until Theresa left home, and then we each had a separate room.

The landing that led upstairs also divided the dining area from the bathroom that had a claw-foot tub barely big enough to hold me, a stool, and a small sink. Try to imagine washing long hair in a sink. It was awful. The kitchen sink was off-limits for that sort of thing. Mother never bought conditioner, which I am sure we did not even know about, so our hair was always dry and unruly. As long as we braided it, it was not much of a problem. But when I wanted to wear my hair loose in a ponytail, the frizz took a few days to calm down. Needless to say, we did not wash our hair often. Theresa and Rosi cut their hair several years before I did and had fewer problems. Mom encouraged me to keep my long hair until I was older.

Next to the kitchen/dining area was the living room with an upright piano, couch, chairs, and our first television. A large area rug provided some warmth and comfort. Another room adjoining the living room through a wide doorway was Mom and Dad's bedroom separated only by a heavy curtain.

This was our home for almost ten years.

In the fall, Rosi and I changed schools again for grades seven and eight. Saint Anthony's grade school and church were located just three or four blocks from our home, and getting there was an easy walk. In addition to weekly student Mass, Rosi and I attended Mass on Sundays even when Mom and Dad did not attend, so living close to the church was a real benefit. I think they did not feel part of the parish community and often chose to stay at home. However, Mom prayed the rosary a lot. She had an incredible memory for feast days—days dedicated to certain saints—and I know she prayed to most of them.

The neighborhood had many children from immigrant Italian families, and we had fun playing hopscotch, tag, and other games. During the summer after my seventh or eighth grade year, I learned to play softball in the park across the street from our house. I actually was a pitcher. I knew nothing about softball when I was asked to join the team. I had not seen it played before, and I was totally unfamiliar with such a common and popular American sport. We did not have a television for a long time, and when we finally bought one, we did not watch sports or develop interest in baseball, basketball, or football.

Just a block from my house, an Italian man opened an ice cream shop during the summer, and I had the opportunity to help some days. Scooping ice cream into cones seems simple, but it was not easy. The ice cream was frozen so hard that I couldn't scrape off more than a thin layer at a time instead of a large scoop full. The owner kept showing me how to do it, but I never did make a tall, beautifully shaped cone like he did.

One classmate I spent a lot of time with was Jo Anna. She had three older brothers. The family members must have had good appetites and eaten a lot of bread because I went to the grocery store with her almost daily to buy at least three loaves. I marveled at how much she purchased on a regular basis.

A relative of Jo Anna's owned a small grocery store just past the ice cream shop, and we often stopped there so she could help herself to big green olives out of a huge barrel. They were shipped in from Italy and kept well for weeks. I disliked the bitter taste from my first bite and have not developed much of a taste for them to this day—except for black olives, which I did not find out about until years later. My walks with Jo Anna helped me to get to know the neighborhood much better than I would have otherwise.

We had good times. Dad was a storyteller and jokester and liked to entertain friends at our home. He enjoyed playing the concertina, an instrument similar to an accordion but with buttons on both sides instead of keys. When friends came to visit, the house was filled with lively music, the carpet was rolled out of the way, and we danced to polkas and waltzes. From an early age, my sisters and I learned to dance because our parents and other adults took us to the dance floor and taught us. We grew up with the beat of music in our blood and bones.

Music and friends provided an important contrast to my parents' daily lives. Dad worked at a packing plant, Bookey Packing Company, where cattle and hogs were butchered. I visited only once, but the visit gave me a good idea of what Dad did there. I walked up a ramp until I stood above the cattle in the pen below me. One by one, the cattle were herded down a chute. A man with a stun gun zapped the animals, and they fell down, unconscious. Other men grabbed the animals with hooks and chains, lifted them up, and cut their throats. After the animals were eviscerated, skinned, and cut in half, the carcasses were hung in coolers for several days to cure. It was hard work bending over and cutting meat all day long. One day, Dad sliced through the little finger of his right hand. It was bent for the rest of his life.

Mother cleaned houses for people, sometimes for as little as a dollar an hour. She finally was hired at a factory in the downtown area that made leather goods. For eight hours a day, she stood bent over a table where she stretched pieces of leather by hand, positioned them just right, and then reached for a die (a metal device used for cutting, forming, or stamping material) hanging above her head. The die hit the leather forcefully and cut it into shapes for gloves, shoes, and other items. Stretching the leather was essential so that when it was sewn into gloves, for example, the leather expanded some but kept its shape.

I visited the factory once and came to appreciate the hard work Mom had to do. Unfortunately, she developed internal bleeding and other physical ailments because of it.

Dad went through a wrestling craze. In the 1950s, wrestling and boxing were popular sports, and Dad got hooked on the wrestling show on TV with Glorious George and other favorites of his. Every week, he became so hyped that he could not sit in his chair but paced the floor and yelled at the TV, the refs, and the men in the ring as if they could hear him and cared. Finally, he attended a wrestling match in person with some friends. He came home disappointed and discouraged. He realized for the first time that what he saw on TV was staged and not the real thing. After that, he no longer looked forward to World Wide Wrestling as he had.

We got along well with our neighbors, but sometimes I wondered what they thought of us. One fall, Dad decided to smoke meat in the garage, and he hung chunks of pork from the rafters. In a bucket below the meat, he lit a fire that smoldered for days and smoked it. The smoke oozed out around the windows and the door. A neighbor who feared the garage was on fire called the police. No one was at home when they came, so they went to the garage and tried to figure out what was going on. You can imagine their surprise when they opened the door. The smoke was so thick they could not see anything until they finally discovered the bucket and the meat hanging above it. Dad was told not to do that again.

The city of Des Moines had both a YMCA and a YWCA. The YWCA hosted a number of programs for foreigners. We went there to socialize as well as to take classes to learn English and to prepare for citizenship. We had to live in America five years before we could apply. As the time drew closer, we were more and more excited as well as hesitant, wondering if we would pass the required test. Mom and

Dad studied hard to learn the names of the first president of the United States, the name of the current president in office, and the American form of government. Since Theresa was an adult by this time, she had to take the test as well. Rosi and I, being minors, qualified under our parents. Of course everyone passed, and we celebrated our new status as American citizens in 1957.

Through mutual friends, Mom and Dad found out that the Pragovich family they had known in Croatia was living in south Chicago and invited them to visit us in Des Moines. Their son Anthony (Tony) and Theresa connected immediately, and after she made a brief visit to Chicago, they decided to marry. They met in May, and their wedding day was in July 1955. They are still married today in 2013.

Saint Joseph Academy

After graduating from eighth grade in 1956, Rosi and I attended Saint Joseph Academy, a Catholic all-girls school. Most of the girls from Saint Anthony's went to Saint Joseph Academy, and the boys attended Dowling High School. Those who chose the public high school went to Lincoln High not far away. Saint Joseph's, on the other hand, was on the west side of Des Moines.

I remember nuns from Saint Joe's coming to our home to encourage my parents to send Rosi and me there even though we would have to pay tuition. We also found out that the students wore uniforms. The reason for this was to de-emphasize differences among the girls, especially when it came to clothing, so there was no need to worry about the latest fashions. That turned out to be a good thing for me because of my limited wardrobe. It relieved me of the need to spend money on clothes in order to fit in with the girls. I did not complain much to Mother, and I don't think she realized how uncomfortable and stressed I felt whenever I had to go somewhere. Often I stood at my closet for long minutes deciding what to wear, not because I had too many choices but because I did not have enough. I could not wear the same outfit twice a week or more, so I had to mix and match. It was difficult to make an outfit look both good and different.

The nuns assured Mom and Dad that Rosi and I would get a good education and grounding in the Catholic faith. Whatever they said convinced Mom and Dad to spend the money to provide us with an opportunity for schooling that they themselves never had.

Rosi dropped out of school after her first year because of language and curriculum challenges. She was old enough to get a job, so she worked at Lindfelt Glove Company and at Des Moines Glove Company for a time and was married in 1961.

Since we had only one car, I took public transportation to get to school. I boarded a bus one block from home and transferred downtown to a bus that took me west to Thirty-Second Street and Grand Avenue. I did this every day for four years loaded down with books and a violin.

How I got the violin is an interesting story. At some point, Rosi and I had started taking piano lessons, which I think we continued throughout most of my high school years. I still enjoy looking at the few pictures we have of the two of us playing duets. I don't remember when we stopped lessons or why, but I have often wished that I had played longer since I enjoyed it so much. However, when I decided to join the school orchestra, I could not play the piano well enough. The band director did not need another drummer, so I started taking violin lessons and muddled my way through four years of band sitting next to Judy, the talented first-chair violinist. I was totally astonished when Rosi gave me a violin as a Christmas gift during my sophomore year, and so I continued with lessons until I graduated.

I certainly got the best education possible at Saint Joseph Academy. The sisters of the Presentation of the Blessed Virgin Mary (PBVMs) were excellent teachers with strict rules and high expectations. I often heard people comment how well educated Saint Joe's grads were. The school was located on several hilly acres on the west side of Des Moines. The school itself was a well-kept older brick building with narrow hallways. To accommodate all the students and move us from class to class swiftly and smoothly, the principal decided that we should walk on the left side of the hallways. To help us remember, we chanted, "Keep to the left, and you'll always be right." I guess it worked, and to this day, I remember that refrain.

Behind the school was a wooded area, and down the slope in a clearing was a lovely grotto with a statue of the Blessed Virgin Mary. We could go there at any time, but one day in the year was special: May Crowning. May 1 in the Catholic calendar of saints is the Feast of the Blessed Virgin Mary. We honored her by processing to the grotto, singing songs to Mary, and then placing a wreath of flowers on her head. One girl, dressed in white, was chosen to lead us. We recited the rosary and then returned to class.

The school song was sung to the tune of "Seventy-six Trombones." It seemed to fit the students of Saint Joe's and our positive outlook very well. Here is just the first verse:

> Thundering forth like jets into outer space
> With adventuresome hearts desiring to dare
> We carry the white and gold into distant lands untold
> And dispel the darkness everywhere.

When yearbooks became available, especially at the end of my senior year, we had some silly traditions. I don't know what students in other schools did, but we signed dozens of books. Of course, we ran out of new and creative things to say, so many of us wrote mundane, repetitive sayings like the following:

> U R
> 2 Nice
> <u>2 Be</u>
> 4 gotten

In 1959, the academy started the first drill team I ever knew about. The girls looked lovely in their pleated skirts sporting the school colors of gold and white. They performed at Dowling, the boys' high school,

Drake University, and Iowa State University and brought the school much attention.

Some girls, of course, became cheerleaders for the boys' games. I enjoyed their cheering very much, perhaps more than some I have witnessed since then. I remember one cheer in particular, even though the words here don't come across as very rousing without the accompanying gestures and voices.

> Go back, go back, go back to the woods,
> You haven't, you haven't, you haven't got the goods.
> You haven't got the rhythm, and you haven't got the jazz.
> You haven't got anything our team has.

I did not participate in many school activities. Saint Joe's had only intramural sports, and these were limited. Dowling, the all-boys school, was across town, and I very infrequently attended games. Mom and Dad simply did not understand American culture well and were not into sports, so going to games was not a focus. I was a loner and spent most of my time studying late into the evening and on weekends. When a math teacher assigned practice problems, I did all of them and more. I kept rewriting essays and research papers many times until I was satisfied. I diagrammed dozens of sentences. That, I believe, formed my understanding of the structure of the English language. I earned mostly As and Bs. If my parents were happy, I breathed easily.

When I was a senior, the history/social studies teacher encouraged us to submit essays for a contest about what it means to be an American. I actually won, and my essay was published in the *Des Moines Register and Tribune* newspaper. We did not subscribe to the paper, so the only way I knew my name and picture were included was because a family friend noticed the article and congratulated me. I was really surprised. Mom and Dad did not make a big deal of it, so I did not either.

St. Joseph Academy, Des Moines, Iowa, where I attended high school

Balancing Work and Fun

During summer vacation, I was alone most of the time since both older sisters and Mother worked. I did not watch TV during the day either. I worked in the garden, canned many quarts of green beans and other vegetables, cleaned the house, and did the laundry every Monday. Washing laundry does not sound bad until one remembers what it was like in the 1950s.

We had a wringer washer. One machine full of water was used for the entire wash load. I sorted clothes into several piles and started with whites, proceeded to dark clothes, and ended with the dirtiest work clothes. After twenty or thirty minutes of washing, I put each item through the wringer into a rinse tub. After rinsing, I put the clothes through the wringer again and then hung them on clotheslines in the yard. In the winter, the clothes were hung on lines in the basement. I was not finished until the clothes were off the lines and folded. All of one morning and most of an afternoon were taken up with this chore.

While emphasis on work and responsibility was constant, we did have fun. One source of enjoyment was the radio. The 1950s were part of the Golden Age of Radio, when radio programming was at its height. It was the primary form of home entertainment and provided hours of listening fun that was a mixture of great music and daytime serials that later became known as soap operas when television took over. I regularly listened to programs such as *Just Plain Bill, Fibber McGee and Molly, Amos and Andy*, and others I can no longer remember. One time Mom took me to see *Gigi*, a 1958 musical with two of the greatest actors of the day, Leslie Caron and Maurice Chevalier. "Thank Heaven for Little Girls" was a popular song from that movie.

Other fun times consisted of spending nights with a girlfriend, going swimming at Sunset Beach in the summer, or joining family and friends at polka dances. Many other Croatians lived in Des Moines, and the Croatian Club sponsored dances with popular polka bands. My Polish and Latvian friends knew how to polka, waltz, and tango, and we had great times. My best friend was Genia, a Polish girl who lived with her widowed mother on the west side of Des Moines. We came to know each other because of the dances we attended. Genia and I spent many nights at each other's home. We talked, listened to music, and danced. I envied her when the Polish community decided to form a dance group to perform at various functions. The young people had so much fun and looked great in their folk dresses.

I often wondered why we did not have our own group. The national dance of Croatia is the kolo, or circle dance. In the kolo, a group of men and women form a circle on the dance floor and hold hands or place them around each other's waists. All the movement is with the feet; the upper body hardly sways. The basic steps are easy but can be fast-paced and tricky, and there are so many versions depending on the area in which people live in Croatia that no one can possibly master even the most popular ones. A leader starts the group quickly by stepping side-to-side or moving toward the center and back out. Sometimes the leader breaks the chain and leads the group around in a long line by weaving in and out. How I would have loved having a folk dress that represented my family's part of the country.

Three of the most common instruments used for the music are the accordion, concertina, and tambura, a long-necked string instrument that resembles a mandolin. A concertina is an instrument similar to an accordion that has buttons on both sides rather than keys. Dad learned to play a concertina, and I enjoyed listening to him. Even though I never saw Dad dance a kolo, he most certainly knew how. He was a good dancer. No wonder Mom fell in love with him.

We enjoyed not only the old-fashioned dances, but we loved to rock and roll. That was the time of Fats Domino, Frank Sinatra, Dean Martin, Jerry Lewis, Perry Como, Pat Boone, Patti Page, and Elvis Presley, to name a few. Dad did not approve of Elvis, of course, with his moving hips and other manners. It was also the time of bobby socks and penny loafers, poodle skirts, and dressy dresses. Hats and gloves were necessities. Skirt lines were to the knee or below, and no one with a sense of decency wore blue jeans to church or any social event. Our favorite TV programs were *I Love Lucy*, *Gunsmoke*, *The Andy Griffith Show*, and *American Bandstand*.

Downtown Des Moines in the 1950s and 1960s was a superb shopping place. Younkers, on the corner of Seventh and Walnut streets, was one of the major anchors of the town. It occupied much of the block, and multiple floors were filled with everything a person could need or desire. One summer I even worked as a clerk in the third-floor women's department. The fifth floor had a tea room frequented (in my opinion) by wealthy, well-dressed women, and I could not imagine myself ever having lunch there. I would have felt out of place. Not until I was invited to lunch there years later did I realize that the people who ate there were mostly ordinary people, so I did not need to feel excluded.

In addition to Younkers, a huge Ben Franklin store with a lunch counter drew in multitudes. The *Des Moines Register and Tribune* building, Cownie Furs, two movie theaters, many grand hotels, and a variety of eating establishments made the downtown area a great place to shop and have fun.

A tour of the Iowa state capitol with friends was memorable. After we eyeballed the governor's office, the law library, and the two vast legislative chambers, we climbed ninety-nine steps to the narrow interior balcony that rings the dome's lower drum. The view of the floors below with their wild pattern-on-pattern tile work was spectacular. A lookout lantern surmounted the dome and for many years it was open to visitors and could be reached by a long, winding staircase that terminated in a finial 275 feet above the ground. The 360-degree view of Des Moines was worth the climb.

Religious Training

Living on the south side of Des Moines, in Little Italy, and attending Saint Anthony's grade school and Saint Joseph's Academy had many benefits. I got a good grounding in my faith even though it was very traditional and unquestioning. At the academy, students went to religion class as regularly as any other class. We learned much about the history of the Catholic Church and its structure and memorized many prayers and Bible passages even though we did not read the Bible frequently. The reason the church gave for its cautious stance was that Scripture could easily be misunderstood or misinterpreted, so to ensure a "correct" understanding, we simply were encouraged to listen to church teaching.

However, attending these schools also had drawbacks. Surrounded by Catholics, I knew nothing of other Christian faiths until I got to college. Even then my faith was not challenged to any great extent. Those were the years before the Second Vatican Council, that momentous convening of leaders in the Catholic Church in order to update its prayers, practices, and some basic doctrine to bring it into the twentieth century.

Before the changes, Catholic teaching was very much sin-based. Frequent confession and Mass attendance were required. We were taught that being Catholic was the only sure way to heaven, and we were strongly encouraged to marry within our faith and not let ourselves be influenced by the flawed teachings of other religions. I am horrified now to think that at one time I actually avoided walking past a Protestant church located across the street from Saint Anthony's school as if I would be contaminated in some way by its proximity.

Also at that time, people in the pews did not participate much in the liturgy. The priest, facing the altar with his back to the congregation, read the prayers in Latin, and the congregation responded and sang many hymns in Latin. Lay people did not proclaim the Scripture readings, distribute communion, or have much input in parish decisions. We truly were the silent majority.

The Second Vatican Council occurred between 1961 and 1965, and it took some time for documents to be written and disseminated to the laity. By then I was long past high school and religion classes where I might have received a better grounding in the "new" church than was the case. What other parishioners and I learned about the changes came from homilies over a period of months that tried to prepare us for the implementation of new prayers, rituals, and music.

Not much was said about fundamental shifts in Catholic teaching, and it was years before I understood the significance of some of them. The following are just few of the more obvious changes.

* The teaching on limbo, which claimed that un-baptized infants could not go to heaven but to some "in between" place, was eliminated.
* People of other faiths can go to heaven since Christ died for all.
* The church put less emphasis on sin.
* The dignity and rights of laity in the church are fundamental and must be promoted.
* The laity––both men and women—are allowed to be Eucharistic ministers and lectors, and girls are allowed to be altar servers.

After graduating from Saint Joseph Academy, I attended Drake University from 1960 to 1964. Since I had maintained a grade point average of over 3.5, and my teachers strongly recommended college, Dad and Mom were willing to consider that route for me. Drake University in Des Moines was the place of choice because I could live at home and pay only tuition, not room and board.

For another four years, rain or shine, I rode the city bus to school. I transferred to a westbound bus in the downtown area and made it to classes on time. I earned a bachelor of science degree in education with a major in English literature and a minor in social studies. My grade point average was above 3.5.

I can hardly explain the impact going to college had on me. Mom and Dad were always overly strict and protective, and going to an all-girls' high school had also limited my exposure to the real world. Seeing so many students, both men and women, was both exciting and intimidating. In health class the first semester, I learned about family planning and contraception, practices that had never been talked about in high school. Many other ideas challenged or contradicted the teachings of the Catholic Church. The new information, however, did not hit me all at once, so I had time to consider how to incorporate it into my belief system.

Attending class in an auditorium with five hundred other students was unusual for most us, and we really had to pay attention and take good notes. Fortunately, those were skills I had learned at Saint Joe's. Unfortunately, since my parents had never even visited a college campus, they knew nothing about student life or the culture that exists on college campuses, including the Greek system of fraternities and sororities. I knew nothing about them either and chose not to join.

I made one major change within the first month at Drake, however. I cut my hair. During high school, the thought that I should cut my hair had occurred now and then, but since I was surrounded by girls and nuns, I did not consider it important. But college was different. I wore my hair either in a long ponytail or rolled into a bun at the back of my head. I felt odd, out of place; it simply had to go. I went to a beauty shop a block east of the campus. Friends noticed the difference in me the very next day and liked it. I have never regretted it.

In the fall of 1964, I started my first year of teaching eighth-grade English at John Muir Junior High School in Milwaukee, Wisconsin. In 1965, I married my husband, Gary, whom I had met during my last year at Drake. We moved to Carbondale, Illinois, where Gary completed his education at Southern Illinois University. Our daughter, Katherine Ann, was born while we were there.

In the spring of 1967, we moved to Orchard, Iowa, where Gary's parents lived and where his father owned and operated a grain elevator and hardware store. Gary had decided to join his father in the grain business. I was fortunate to be hired to teach eighth-grade English at the junior high school in Osage beginning in the fall of 1967. Our first son, Frank, was born in February 1968, so I was limited to one semester of teaching. Mark was born in October 1969, and Michael came along in June 1971. I put my teaching career on hold for many years since raising our children was more important.

Final Thoughts

According to Mom and Dad, hard work is the path to a better life. They did not expect life to be easy, and I have come to admire and appreciate them for their ability to survive great challenges. Dad deserves credit for his dream and courage to leave everything behind in Austria and embark into an unknown future. I cannot imagine the sense of desperation that led him to such a momentous decision. While our worst years during and after World War II were limited in duration, my family and thousands of others like us were reduced to nothing at some point. No wonder Dad battled demons most of his life that drove him to bouts of alcoholism and frequently inhabited his dreams.

Mom and Dad's inability––or unwillingness––to accept a more liberal American culture certainly impacted my sisters and me. They brought the Old World with them. I am a little surprised at their inflexibility, considering that Mother was only thirty-two years old when we came to America and Dad was thirty-nine. Of course, it took a number of years to learn English, and by that time, they were set in their ways and attitudes.

Without realizing what was happening, we learned to accept harsh circumstances. My sisters and I endured; we knew we could not change our condition. At some point, each one of us did choose her own path, but the underlying attitude of acceptance and resignation operated within us––especially within me. It takes much for me to rock the boat, to take strong action. My first concern is always for the other person. I do not want to hurt or alienate anyone. While I cannot speak for my sisters, I have noticed similar tendencies in them.

Fear and timidity in new situations and relationships plagued me most of my life. People who could talk to anyone about anything and did not seem cowed by authority amazed me. I wish things had been different, but looking back, I realize good things resulted. I developed strong habits of perseverance, hard work, and survival under harsh circumstances. I got a good education that formed the foundation for my success in college. My confidence came from having done well despite many barriers, and it continues to develop as I accept new challenges and responsibilities. I work despite sickness and other inconveniences; I am a go-getter rather than a procrastinator. I will always be introspective and judge myself harshly. However, I have come to accept myself as I am to a large extent, and I believe in the importance of accepting people as they are.

The language spoken within the family circle remained mostly Croatian. After I learned English, I switched to that almost totally, but Mom and Dad did not. That is understandable, but now I regret forgetting so much of my mother tongue, especially after I married and moved from home. I understand more than I can speak, but I know if I were immersed in a group that spoke only Croatian, I would become fluent again before long. I often yearn for opportunities to speak both Croatian and German, but I know I will never lose my knowledge of the basic sound patterns of both, which was of great benefit in learning English. I studied French in high school as well, and I have come to realize that I have a gift for language. I learn words easily and like to write.

However, losing my first language and then my second one before the age of ten has limited my ability to remember or talk about early experiences. Whether we recall them or not, our experiences lay the foundation for our beliefs and hopes, attitudes and behaviors, and even how we love. Forgotten events affect our lives in unconscious ways, so I am grateful that I can intentionally talk about painful events in the hope of lessening their grip on me. I am who I am, and I still struggle to understand and accept all that means. The path has been a difficult one, but we were blessed to come to America. After sixty years, I cannot imagine living anywhere else.

Theresa and Rosi

We often know not how others see us, and our self-perceptions and hang-ups color the truth. We dismiss praise, feelings of satisfaction, and pride, even when we have a right to claim them. My sisters and I were never encouraged to do "our own thing" and enjoy life. We took life seriously and focused on duty. I admire what my sisters have done and have become, and I want to put into words my observations of them and express my love.

Theresa

Because she was the oldest, Theresa often had to be in charge of Rosi and me when our parents were away. From an early age, she was expected to shoulder much responsibility. When I was ten and she only sixteen, she left home to work as a nanny, so we saw her only on weekends. She lived at home during our years in Des Moines and kept learning and moving ahead in various jobs. She married Anthony Pragovich at age nineteen, moved to Chicago, and continued to work to support the family even after their son was born. Theresa and Tony lived with his parents, and Tony's mother took care of Tony Jr.

We did not have much in common in our childhood and early adult years. However, Theresa encouraged and supported me in ways Mom and Dad did not. It was Theresa who told me about becoming a woman just days before my first period. Mother never mentioned anything, before or after the fact, and I did not feel comfortable going to Mother when I had questions or problems. After I had my own family, the bonds between Theresa and me strengthened and deepened. I have always looked up to her and considered her an intelligent, competent, decisive, hardworking person. She also is considerate, loving, and forgiving. The following poem expresses my thoughts best.

To Theresa

This is a poem to you, my sister, Theresa,
Whom I admire more than I can say.
You have borne the burden of too much responsibility.
Out of necessity much was expected of you.
You became strong and confident.
Your scars are the source of your strength.

Do you ever doubt, question?
It seems you always know what to do, know what you want.
You give your all—more than is expected or asked.
Your drive to achieve and shoulder the weight of others
Has often blinded me to your needs.
The world, I have discovered, recognizes not
The needs of those who are strong and walk tall.
Now I see differently.

I have not told you often enough
How generous and special you are,
How much I love you, Theresa, sister of mine.

Rosi

The effects of Rosi's illness when she was a very young child affected her all her life. I don't remember that she was sickly growing up, but her constitution was not as healthy and sturdy as Theresa's or mine. Mom and Dad did not expect as much from her as they did of us. We will never know how her limited abilities and opportunities and lack of encouragement affected her. She became quiet, reserved, and patient yet strong-willed.

She married Joe Grenko, a man many years her senior. Three of their five children were born learning disable in varying degrees, and Joe died when the youngest was only eight. Rosi had to work and raise them alone with little family support since Mom and Dad moved from Des Moines to Chicago and Theresa and I were also gone and focused on our own lives. I never heard her complain about the challenges she faced during those years. She, too, like the rest of my family, is a survivor. As happened with Theresa, Rosi and I became closer as we grew older and reached out to each other. I love her deeply. Here is my tribute to her.

To a Rose

The garden where you rooted was not conducive to growth.
You sprouted like the others, but already in and around you
Were hidden the conditions that formed you different.
Development was arrested. Oh, by how many forces?

Gardeners who tended you prodded, pruned, neglected.
You surrounded yourself with a hard protective layer
And hid within your heart much beauty and potential,
Stunted before their time.

Petals—small, singed, tight—entrap the greatness within.
Rarely do you allow others to glimpse fears, doubts,
Hopes, desires that still flicker deep in your soul.
No one knows what burdens you bear,
What sorrows break your heart.

Few give you credit for surviving many odds.
You are sensitive, generous, gladdened by small things.
You give much, accept much, ask for little in return.
Be proud. Be strong. A bud has a beauty all its own.

Epilogue

My many years as a wife, mother of four, teacher, friend, and volunteer deserve a book of their own. The focus in this book, however, has been on my early foundational years.

Our formative years affect us in ways we cannot fathom, not only ourselves but also our spouses and children and others with whom we come in contact. Attitudes and tendencies are subtle characteristics that we take for granted and overlook in ourselves. Acceptance and forgiveness are essential to seeing both strengths and weaknesses in others and choosing to focus on the gifts and graces people possess. This allows us to appreciate them, recognize their value, and reach out in compassion. It is the way of peace.

Appendix

Pictures in Croatia

Mom and Dad holding Theresa, my oldest sister, standing by our farmhouse in Voćin

Dad in military uniform

Family picture (probably early years in Lahrndorf, Austria)

Pictures in Austria

Grandpa and Grandma Wahl and Girls in Austria

Theresa, Rosi, and Margaret

**Margaret's class picture, grade 2 or 3, in Garsten.
Row 2, second from left.**

Pictures taken early 1950s in Austria:

Frank Grguric (Dad)

Theresa Grguric (Mom)

Theresa Grguric (oldest sister)

Rose Grguric (middle sister)

Margaret Grguric

Des Moines, Iowa

Dad playing concertina in Des Moines

Illinois

Theresa, back row, far right, member of Kolo Club in Illinois, wearing Croatian national costume, 2014.

CPSIA information can be obtained at www.ICGtesting.com
Printed in the USA
LVOW10*0036120914

403706LV00003B/23/P

9 781490 840345